MARBLE &

REDSTONE
A Quick History

By Jim Nelson

Cover illustration of Redstone Castle, Redstone Inn, and Marble Community Church by Sam Thiewes

Published by *Blue Chicken* PUBLISHING
1512 Grand Avenue, Glenwood Springs, CO 81601

Printed in the United States

ISBN 1-928971-02-4

TABLE OF CONTENTS

CHAPTER 1

THE FORMATION OF "TREASURE MOUNTAIN DOME"

Many millions of years ago, the appearance of the earth was quite different from what we see today. Massive continent-sized chunks of land, called tectonic plates, make up the earth's crust. The plates float on the surface of the magma, the molten rock which makes up the core of the earth. Due to forces that are not completely understood, the plates move. They move very slowly and ponderously, but they do move. All of the continents and the sea floors are part of the plates system, and to this day, they continue to move and spread.

Some scientists believe that, some 225 million years ago, the land areas of our planet were combined in a supercontinent which they refer to as Pangea. Others subscribe to the hypothesis that there were two huge continents, the Northern Hemisphere continent of Laurasia, and Gondwanaland in the Southern Hemisphere, separated by the Tethys Sea. The two theories agree, however, that the movement of the plates eventually split the continents. The rift widened over the millennia, forming the Atlantic Ocean.

The tectonic plates continued to move. As the movements brought two of the plates together, one might have ridden up over the other, or the edges may have been pushed upwards. Massive uplifts, caused by these movements, resulted in huge mountain ranges. These jagged peaks stood proudly for great spans of time, but all of them eventually became victims of erosion. The relentless actions of wind and water, aided by the irresistible force of gravity, have reduced all but the youngest of the mountain ranges to tiny specks of sand. In many cases, these specks were washed away by melting snows and torrents of rainwater to some ancient sea. As the remnants of the ancient rock settled to the bottom of the seas, they formed layers. Each new layer of sediment covered the older layers, adding weight and pressure. This pressure would eventually transform the grains of sand into newer sedimentary rock.

A cross-section of ancient sedimentary rock in the Marble area, showing the layers which were gradually hardened into rock by pressure and heat, and later tilted by the forces of volcanic activity. (Photo by the author)

As the remains of the ancestral mountain ranges slowly filtered down and reformed into layers of rock, the plates continued to wander. The slow but persistent movements resulted in earthquakes, the covering or uncovering of volcanic vents, and the fracturing and elevating of the edges of the plates. In some instances, the broken edges were pushed many thousands of feet into the air. It was just such an uplift that formed the Ancestral Rockies, an enormous mountain range that once existed approximately where the present Rocky Mountains now stand. Geologists estimate that the Ancestral Rockies may have reached 35,000 feet in elevation. The sediment from those peaks now covers most of Colorado and Utah, as well as parts of Nebraska and Kansas, with red sandstone.

Sometime prior to 300 million years ago, a warm, shallow sea covered much of what is now Colorado. The waters were home to some really bizarre experiments in the evolution of fish, as well as a form of shark that may have reached 50 feet in length. There also existed many billions of tiny creatures, whose lot it was to provide the bulk of the food chain as it existed in those days. Not content to submit to indiscriminate consumption by all comers without offering at least some resistance, many of these tiny organisms did a little evolving on their own. They developed tiny shells for protection. The shells were made up of a mineral called calcium carbonate, and were so hard that they usually outlasted their occupant. Many millions of years later, scientists would know the creatures and their surviving descendants as crustaceans.

As each of the little hard-shelled organisms went to their reward, the abandoned shells and the accompanying skeletons settled to the bottom of the sea, forming layers many feet thick. As other sediments covered them, the pressure compacted the shells, gradually changing them to a rock called limestone. Limestone is a fine-grained rock made up of calcite from the ancient shells. Much of central Colorado was covered by a formation which has come to be known as "Leadville Limestone". It got its name from limestone deposits around and under Leadville, Colorado, which were found to contain rich deposits of lead, zinc, and especially silver. The ores were igneous intrusions into the limestone, creating pockets of the metals.

In a very few places on earth, combinations of water, pressure, and heat from volcanic activity have worked to dramatically change the crystalline structure of limestone deposits. When this happens, the tiny calcite crystals change, or metamorphose, into larger sparkling crystals. The new rock is harder, more compact, and tends to exhibit a luster. In its purest form, where the heat of the earth's crust was the hottest, it is pure white in color. It is known as marble.

Chair Mountain - "igneous intrusion" at the upper end of the Crystal River Valley - formed when volcanic magma forced its way upwards, elevating the overlaying layers of rock. The overlayment has since eroded away, revealing the surviving granite. (Courtesy of Frontier Historical Society - Shutte Collection)

Some 60 million years ago, a rather dramatic upheaval along the spine of the North American continent pushed up what was to become the present day Rocky Mountains. This particular uplift was accompanied by a great deal of volcanic activity. Mount Sopris, which sits at one end of the Elk Mountains not far from the confluence of the Crystal River with the Roaring Fork River, is an example of what is known as an igneous intrusion. It was formed when molten rock, or magma, forced its way upwards. The intrusion of magma never broke the surface of the ground to become a volcano. Rather, it solidified after pushing up the overlaying rock and earth. That overlayment has long since eroded away, revealing the harder igneous core of the mountain that can be seen today.

Mount Sopris, volcanic "igneous intrusion" at the lower end of the Crystal River Valley. (Courtesy of Frontier Historical Society - Shutte Collection)

As Mount Sopris was forming, another intrusion a few miles to the south was also producing massive amounts of magma. This intrusion happened to be under a thick bed of the Leadville Limestone. The tremendous pressure elevated, or "domed" the limestone layer. At the same time, the heat of the magma metamorphosed the limestone into marble. Most of the organic matter, which had colored the limestone black, was burned away. Much of the dome of marble that remained was of the purest white. The dome is some seven miles in diameter, and has come to be known as the Treasure Mountain Dome.

Treasure Mountain, a massive dome of marble formed when beds of limestone were pushed upwards by volcanic activity. (Courtesy of Frontier Historical Society - Shutte Collection)

Like Mount Sopris, the igneous rocks under the dome of marble pushed up the rocks and earth which lay above it. Much of that material has been eroded away, but enough remains to camouflage the dome. Thus, there is no huge, gleaming knob of white marble to attract the eye. However, enough of the white rock shows on the surface of the mountain slopes to provide a hint of what lies beneath.

CHAPTER 2

THE ORIGINAL INHABITANTS OF THE CRYSTAL RIVER VALLEY

The Ute Indians controlled much of the central Rocky Mountain area for many hundreds of years, but they were not the first inhabitants. The first humans to venture into what was to become known as the Crystal River Valley were the Paleo-Indians, the earliest occupants of the North American Continent. These Ancient peoples originally crossed into the "new world" on a now submerged land bridge from Northern Asia some 18,000 to 20,000 years ago. They spent the next few thousand years spreading across North and South America. They were relatively few in number, and they left little evidence of their passing. However, their stone tools and projectile points, along with fossilized bones from their kill sites, reveal that they were quite accomplished hunters. Their prey in those days consisted of woolly mammoths, giant sloths, camels, and a form of horse. In fact, the extinction of all of these animals on this continent may have been partly due to their use by the Paleo-Indians as sources of food, clothing, and other materials.

Most of the Colorado sites attributed to the Paleo-Indians are on the eastern plains. However, evidence exists that they moved through the mountains of the western part of the state, probably on a seasonal basis. Like the Utes who came later, the early people were hunter-gatherers. They followed the annual ripening of the nuts and berries, the migration patterns of the elk, the deer, the mountain buffalo. They likely vacated the upper reaches of the Crystal River Valley in the winter, due to deep snows and frigid temperatures.

There is no record of the ultimate fate of the Paleo-Indians. It is generally accepted that they were the ancestors of many of the Indian tribes that came later. They became the Aztec and Toltec of South America, the Makah of the Pacific

9

Northwest, the Apache of the Southwestern deserts. They were the forefathers of the Anasazi, who were in turn the forefathers of the modern Pueblo Indians of New Mexico. They are probably the ancestors of the Utes, but no record of that lineage exists. Efforts have been made to establish a direct connection between the ancient inhabitants of the Uncompahgre Plateau of Western Colorado and the Ute Indians who lived there during the past few hundred years. No such connection has as yet been made. According to the theory of at least one member of the Ute Mountain Ute Tribe, the modern Utes migrated to the Colorado area from far to the south. He bases his hypothesis on the fact that there is a word for "monkey" in the Ute ancient language.

Ute Camp with teepee and hunting stand. (Courtesy of Frontier Historical Society)

Whereas many of the more recent, or "historic" Indian tribes gradually turned to farming, the cultivation of crops and forms of irrigation for at least part of their subsistence, the Utes never moved beyond the hunter-gatherer stage. The country in which they lived, the mesas and canyons of the mountain west, demanded that they continue to move with the seasons. The high mountain meadows, so inviting and game-filled in the summers and early fall, became wastelands of snow and ice and bitter winds in the winter. The pinon nuts and wild grains matured at different times in different locations and altitudes. When the "grocery store" for a people is spread over several hundred square miles, survival depends upon movement.

Trappers Lake in the Flattops Wilderness Area - part of the land originally controlled by the Ute Indians. (Photo by the author)

The Utes were not a particularly warlike people, but they jealously guarded their "territory". Surrounding tribes, the Shoshone and the Apache and the Comanche and others, admired the area controlled by the Utes. The plentiful herds of game, the abundant water supplies, and the occasional hot mineral springs attracted the attention of the neighbors. However, less than 10,000 Utes held control of most of Colorado and Utah and parts of Wyoming and New Mexico for several hundred years.

The Utes survived quite nicely for many centuries on foot. Like many of the other North American tribes, they did not acquire the horse until sometime in the 1600's. As mentioned, the Paleo-Indians presumably ate the last of the "American" horses many years previously. Thanks to the Spanish who established residency in the Santa Fe, New Mexico area, the Utes were able to "borrow" a few ponies here and there. They became excellent horsemen, and horses

Two members of the Ute Indian Tribe - picture taken about 1898. (Courtesy of Frontier Historical Society)

gradually became a measure of wealth for the members of the tribe.

The White River band of the Utes lived in the Roaring Fork River and the Crystal River Valley for at least part of each year. The volcanic vents which produced such geological phenomena as Mount Sopris and Treasure Mountain Dome never fully closed. The remaining ducts continued to release not molten rock, but hot mineral water. The Yampah Springs which feed the Hot Springs Pool and the vapor caves in Glenwood Springs are the most prominent examples of these geothermal vents. The Siloam Springs at the east end of Glenwood Canyon and the Penny Hot Springs between Carbondale and Redstone also warmed and relaxed the Ute people. They considered the healing mineral waters to be a gift from Manitou, their God. Like the rest of the Ute territory, the hot springs were coveted by other tribes, and more than one battle was waged over possession of them. The Utes maintained ownership for hundreds of years, but it was not to last.

When the Civil War ended in the 1860's, thousands of would-be prospectors headed toward the Rocky Mountains. They sought gold and silver, copper, zinc, and lead. Denver became a jumping-off place for these fortune hunters, and the fact that the mountains just to the west "belonged" to the Ute Indians was looked upon as nothing more than an irritant. The Utes met most of the very early intruders with a degree of friendliness. Richard Sopris, the man for whom the mountain is named, came to the area in 1860. He became ill, and the local Utes recommended that he be taken to the healing hot springs at the confluence of the Roaring Fork, then known as the Thunder River, and the Colorado River, then called the Grand. Sopris thus became the first documented white man to use the sacred hot springs of the Utes.

As the influx of eager prospectors increased, so did the resentment of the Utes. As with many other tribes, the United States government signed treaties with the Utes, guaranteeing them, among other things, the right to possess portions of Western Colorado "for as long as the rivers might run and grasses might grow." In turn, the Indians promised to recognize the jurisdiction of the U.S. government. Many of the prospectors routinely ignored the agreements, and continued to encroach on Ute lands in their efforts to "strike it rich".

"The Utes Must Go!" became the rallying cry of the ever-increasing white population, a sentiment which was echoed by major newspapers. They were looked upon as a nuisance, an impediment to "progress". The government continued to reduce the amount of land upon which the Utes were allowed to live and hunt. To a people who had always roamed freely throughout the mountains of Western Colorado and Utah, the restrictions were abhorrent.

Colorow, White River Ute Chieftain at the time of the ouster of the Ute Tribe from the Crystal River and Roaring Fork River valleys. (Courtesy of Frontier Historical Society)

On September 29, 1879, a relatively small group of White River Utes gave the white man the excuse that was needed to evict the tribe from Western Colorado. In response to what they considered to be totally unreasonable demands by Nathan Meeker, the Indian Agent for the White River Utes, they attacked and killed Meeker and many of his men. They also kidnapped several women, including Meeker's wife and daughter, and ambushed an army detail which was on its way to the agency. In outrage over what was to be called the Meeker Massacre, the government forced the Utes to relocate to a reservation in Eastern Utah. The Utes were allowed to return to their former hunting grounds each summer for a few years, but even that was not to last.

Sign commemorating the Meeker Massacre near Meeker, Colorado. (Photo by the author)

With the Utes out of the way, the mountains of Colorado were finally open to the prospectors and the homesteaders. They came into the valley of the marble dome from all directions; over Cottonwood Pass and across the Roaring

Fork River, down the Roaring Fork valley from Aspen, across Schofield Pass, and over McClure Pass from the west. They had their eyes to the ground, searching for a trace of the minerals which had brought them to the area. Most of them walked right past the huge marble deposits of the Treasure Mountain Dome.

Legend has it that, as the Ute Indians were being removed from what was to become known as the Crystal River Valley against their will, they put a "curse" on the area. They declared that the white man would never prosper in the valley. Whether this in fact happened is a matter for debate. It is just possible that Frank Frost, editor of the *Marble Booster*, started the legend in 1917, when Marble was experiencing some difficult times.

CHAPTER 3

THE PROSPECTORS ARRIVE

Several generations of Ute Indians saw the occasional white man wander through the area that was to become known as the Crystal River Valley. Don Juan Rivera, on a 1765 mission to explore the wilderness north of New Mexico, traveled close to, and perhaps into, the valley. In 1776, The Spanish Fathers Dominguez and Escalante passed just to the west in their effort to chart a route from Santa Fe to Monterey, California. From the 1830's through the early 1850's, the only whites in the valley were the mountain men, the beaver trappers.

The Crystal River below Marble. Much of the year, the river lives up to its name.
(Photo by the author)

After the Civil War ended, the mountain west saw the influx of thousands of prospectors. Explorer and prospector William Gant worked his way up Rock Creek, the original name of the Crystal River, in 1859. He reported finding an old, rusted gold pan some three miles below the future site of Marble. It was theorized that a few of the "49ers" may have panned the valley on their way to the gold rush in California.

Benjamin Graham and six other prospectors set up camp at the head of Rock Creek in 1870. They discovered some anthracite coal and galena, a lead ore which often also contains silver. Ignoring the fact that it was still Ute territory, they built a cabin and outbuildings, and settled in. In 1874, the Utes burned the buildings and drove the trespassers out.

A member of a geological survey group from Denver, Sylvester Richardson, was the first to recognize the value of the outcroppings of white marble on the slopes above the river. He did little more than record its existence, however, and it was up to George Yule, prospector and later sheriff of Gunnison County, to "rediscover" it in 1874. The creek which runs down through the marble deposits became known as Yule Creek. However, it was still not the sparkling white rock that excited the imagination. Some 14 miles to the southeast of the Marble area in the Schofield Pass vicinity, traces of silver, gold, copper, zinc, and lead were showing up. The ouster of the Utes in 1879 opened the mountains to "development", and the town of Schofield soon boasted sixty or so houses, a store, a hotel, and several saloons. The little town boomed until 1885, when it was basically abandoned. The winter of 1883-1884 was unusually harsh, even for the Colorado high country. Most of the residents moved some four miles down to Crystal.

Significant gold and silver deposits had been discovered at Crystal, as well as some beautiful silicon crystals. They were the source of the name for the town, and Rock Creek was renamed the Crystal River in 1886. As the hills around

18

Crystal became patched with mining claims, newcomers and the more unsuccessful of the prospectors moved on down the valley toward the huge dome of marble.

Crystal City - once a booming mining town, now deserted much of the year. Accessible for four-wheel-drive road. (Courtesy of Frontier Historical Society - Shutte Collection)

As John Mobley and his wife topped Schofield Pass on their way to the future site of Marble, their donkey broke loose. It disappeared down the trail, carrying not only their provisions, but also their two children, Nellie and Chet. The children were in panniers, twin bags which rode on the sides of the pack animal. The burro was finally stopped far down the trail by another miner named William Woods. The children somehow escaped the misadventure unscathed.

Mobley and W. F. Mason founded the town of Clarence in 1881. Not long after, William Woods and William Parry formed the town of Marble just to the west.

In the early 1880's, efforts were made to interest the world in the massive marble deposits, but silver and other metals still demanded the attention of most of the residents. Finally, in 1884, the first marble quarry in the Crystal River Valley was opened by a man named Howell. His quarry was located some distance upstream from Crystal. Then, in 1885 and 1886, four quarries were opened on Yule Creek, much closer to Marble.

It was becoming more and more obvious that they had tapped into an almost inexhaustible supply of marble. However, there was a great deal of labor involved in processing the heavy stone. That required money, which was not a plentiful commodity among the early developers; in July of 1886, John Cleveland Osgood solved that problem. Osgood was a principle in both the Colorado Midland Railroad and the White Breast Fuel Company, and he purchased bonds, or options, to several of the marble claims. This allowed the quarry operators to process the marble into manageable shapes. The problem then centered around shipping the extremely heavy blocks. There was no railroad, no highway, not even a decent wagon road either down the Crystal River Valley to Carbondale or over Schofield Pass to Crested Butte.

Even though James J. Hagerman, another principle in the Colorado Midland Railroad, acquired the deeds to some forty-one acres of marble claims in 1886, the 1880's were to come to a close without appreciable progress in railroad building in the valley. Interest in the marble deposits was gradually increasing, however. Yule marble had been proposed for the floors of the new State Capitol in Denver, and outsiders were investing in the marble claims to the tune of tens of thousands of dollars.

In January of 1890, the town of Marble filed an application for a post office. Neighboring Clarence also filed the same application. The two towns competed for almost two years before Marble finally won out. At that time, most of the mining operations ceased when winter hit, as 200 inches of snowpack was not uncommon. Even so, the little towns each had a number of year-round residents.

Activity continued to increase during the spring of 1890. In July, a syndicate from Denver purchased the Yule Creek quarries. They promoted the quality of the marble to architects and contractors, most of whom expressed enthusiasm. However, the continued lack of adequate transportation was still the major stumbling block to development. Steven Keene, the organizer of the syndicate, convinced the Denver and Rio Grande Western Railroad to survey a route from Crested Butte over Yule Pass to Marble. Finding grades of up to 10 percent, the D&RGW decided against the project.

In 1891, John Osgood reappeared on the scene, acquiring deeds to several of the quarries which he had earlier bonded. Osgood, by now one of the richest men in Colorado, was to exhibit a block of marble from one of these claims at the Columbian Exposition in Chicago in 1893. Also, Steven Keene obtained the financial support which he had been seeking, and became general manager of the Colorado Marble and Mining Company. The new company determined that, "The Yule Creek deposits will supply the world for every purpose for 400 years." They stated that they would build a railroad from the upper end of the quarries to Crested Butte, and were prepared to spend $150,000 on the project. An electric tram railway, considered more suitable for the steep grades, was planned. They planned to begin construction of the railroad in the spring of 1892.

Meanwhile, Stephen Keene brought in potential buyers from the east coast of the United States and even from Italy. With the increased potential, plans were made to build another railroad from Carbondale up the Crystal River Valley to Marble. It seemed that Marble was finally poised on the brink of the long-anticipated boom. There still wasn't a decent wagon road to the quarries, but two railroads were planned, and the residents of the area waited anxiously.

In early 1892, the post office was awarded to Marble. Some say that a Dr. Robert H. Kline, who then owned a half interest in the Marble townsite, was a personal friend of John Wanamaker, the Postmaster General. Whatever the reason, Marble and Clarence combined on July 4, 1892. The name of Marble survived.

The spring of 1892 came and went, with no sign of the promised railroad to Crested Butte. The Colorado Marble and Mining Company then announced that a wagon road would be constructed, and that it would be the forerunner of the actual tram, which would be built later. Late in 1892 Stephen Keene announced that, had the wagon road been completed, his company could have sold $500,000 worth of marble. The year of 1892 closed as it had opened, with numerous quarries in operation and almost no progress in the development of a reasonable transportation method for the blocks of marble.

In 1893, silver was abandoned by the U.S. Government as backing for its currency. The value of silver plummeted overnight. Fortunes evaporated and miners found themselves staring at now almost worthless mines that had promised riches the day before. Towns such as Leadville, Aspen, and Crystal emptied as the stunned miners abandoned them.

Marble was not greatly effected by the Silver Panic of 1893, as enthusiasm was still high. So many promises of transportation corridors had been made by then that it seemed logical that at least one of them would come into existence. A white marble column, quarried by Keene's company, was sent to the Columbian Exposition to join the block of marble sent there by Osgood. Both companies took orders for marble at the exposition, confident that the boom was at hand. Meanwhile, Dr. Kline was extolling the virtues of Yule marble to the authorities in Denver, stating that it was the only material suitable for the State Capitol floors. The anticipated contract called for 140,000 square feet of marble, and the company which landed it would surely prosper. The exhibits at the exposition had drawn the first prize as the finest marble, and the seemingly boundless optimism continued.

CHAPTER 4

THE OPTIMISM FINALLY SEEMS JUSTIFIED

In 1895, the architects of the State Capitol made the announcement that Yule Marble had been chosen for the floors. Production began immediately, but the transportation problems again reared their head. By November, the State Capitol managers were forced to send a representative to Marble to investigate the cause of delays in shipping. He discovered that the marble was being carried by sled to the railhead at Carbondale. However, the 30 mile wagon

The Colorado State Capitol Building in Denver. The floors of the Capitol building are made of Yule marble. (Photo by the author)

road from Carbondale to Marble was completed shortly thereafter. After years of hope and broken promises, there was finally a reasonable way to transport the beautiful stone.

Colorado Yule marble had been judged to be of the finest quality in the world. Testing had proven that its hardness exceeded even Carrara marble, Italy's best. The marble was there, untold quantities of it. The quarries were in place, poised to produce blocks of the hard, white stone. At long last, there was an actual road down which the stone could be transported. The railroads had not as yet arrived in Marble, but it was only a matter of time.

Interior of the quarry, around 1915. (Courtesy of Frontier Historical Society - Shutte Collection)

The completion of the road seemed to be the catalyst that Marble needed. Although silver had lost its allure, the other ores were plentiful enough to warrant the construction of a smelter in 1897. Prior to that, much of the ore was shipped to Denver or Pueblo for smelting. The availability of the smelter also allowed some of the smaller mines to sell ore directly.

The new road also brought the Crystal River Stage Line to town. It provided passenger and mail service between Marble and Carbondale. A telephone line was planned from Carbondale to Marble and Crystal, but it was not to happen until later.

Then, in August of 1898, the Crystal River Railroad Company announced that they would build a rail line to Marble from Carbondale. The construction actually began, but the winter of 1898-99 was one of the worst on record, and seriously delayed the construction. Between the deep snows and the mudslides of the following spring, work was halted for several months. The marble interests, as well as the miners of the area, waited impatiently. The line had reached Redstone, so it remained to complete the standard gauge track to Marble, and from there a narrow gauge line on up to Crystal. Unfortunately, that was not to happen anytime soon.

Marble residents, all 90 of them, voted to incorporate in 1899. They were thus able to carry out improvements, establish a municipal water system, and elect public officials. Also in 1899, John Osgood and his money reappeared. He formed the Yule Creek White Marble Company, and appointed F. H. Eaton to run it for him. Eaton brought machinery in from New Jersey to work the quarry. The

Marble quarry openings on the side of Treasure Mountain. (Courtesy of Frontier Historical Society - Shutte Collection)

work was slow at first, because many of the early quarry workers had come from the mines, where ore was removed by blasting. Early on, the same methods were used on the marble. They would drill into the marble deposits and set charges to fracture huge chunks of it away from the beds. While crudely effective, the blasting left a deep overburden of cracked marble which had to be removed to reach undamaged deposits. Unfortunately, problems with some of Osgood's other financial ventures were to prevent any degree of success with the Yule Creek White Marble Company.

As the 20th century arrived, the citizens of the upper Crystal River Valley were, as usual, optimistic. The smelter was in operation, some of the mines were producing high-grade ore, and Osgood had not as yet been distracted from

Train caught in a snowslide below Marble - 1907. (Courtesy of Frontier Historical Society)

his marble operation. The railroad had not yet reached Marble. The rich coal deposits at Coal Basin west of Redstone were considered to be more deserving of a rail line than were the marble and ore reserves around Marble. In 1901, Osgood, a major shareholder in the Crystal River Railroad, proposed extending the line from Redstone to Prospect. Prospect was only three miles from Marble, and eventually the line was to be built into Marble itself.

In 1903, John Osgood was at last pulled away from any further involvement in his marble company. He became embroiled in a battle for control of Colorado Fuel and Iron Company, and seldom returned thereafter. However, as he disappeared from the scene, others were waiting in the wings. Marble was about to enter an era of success for which the residents had waited for so long.

Channing Frank Meek, originally from Mt. Pleasant, Iowa, was looked upon by many as the patron saint of Marble. Meek held the honorary title of Colonel, and many knew him by that title. He had held management positions with several railroad companies, and in 1890 he became president of the Colorado Coal and Iron Company. In 1893, he consolidated his company with John Osgood's organization, forming the Colorado Fuel and Iron Company. Osgood came out of that merger as the head of CF&I, so Meek went on to organize the Shredded Wheat Company of Denver and the American Biograph Company. He then purchased the streetcar lines in Mexico City. He converted the lines to electric power and ultimately sold them at a huge profit.

His interest returning to Western Colorado, he focused on the Marble area. He was greatly excited by the prospects of the vast marble deposits, and began acquiring mineral patents which included part of the marble beds. He invested millions of dollars in the area and was responsible for the construction of the marble finishing mill, the largest in the world.

In the early days of marble quarrying in the Crystal River Valley, it was considered more economical to finish

Channing Frank Meek, considered by many to be the patron saint of Marble. He was instrumental in much of the intitial development of the quarries and the marketing of the white stone. (Courtesy of Denver Public Library - Western History Collection)

the marble, slicing or carving it into its final shape, close to the quarry. Thus, Meek's company was able to transport the huge, heavy blocks of marble from the quarry high on the side of Treasure Mountain to his mill, located not quite four miles away in Marble itself. The mill was, for its day, a marvel of mechanical engineering. Overhead cranes loaded and unloaded the railroad cars. The same cranes moved the marble around inside the mill, delivering it to the huge saws and drills which then cut it to the required shapes. Gang saws sliced the blocks into thin sheets, to be used for facing materials for walls or floors. Old World craftsmen from Italy, Austria, and other European countries performed their art on the stone, transforming it into sparkling, smooth, white treasures.

Interior of the world's largest marble processing mill, showing the overhead crane and work in progress. Photo from about 1910. (Courtesy of Frontier Historical Society)

A Montrose newspaper editor by the name of Adams wrote:

"The machinery was as big as all outdoors. I never before saw such a massive plant. Machinery until you could not rest. Such a noise and hum you could scarcely hear yourself think. Great cranes were carrying great blocks of marble as easily as though they were pebbles. There were giant saws cutting huge blocks in two, and every machine conceivable to cut and trim marble into the shape desired. The saws and planers run in water to keep them cool and at the same time soften the stone a trifle. Great blocks of marble are brought in at one end of the building and when they go out the other they are finished and polished and carved and crated or boxed ready to be loaded upon the cars."

In February of 1905, the Colorado-Yule Marble Company was incorporated. Meek shortly acquired both the control and the presidency of the new company. By November

The "Black Bull," a giant rotary snowplow that was used to clear the tracks between Carbondale and Marble. (Courtesy of Frontier Historical Society)

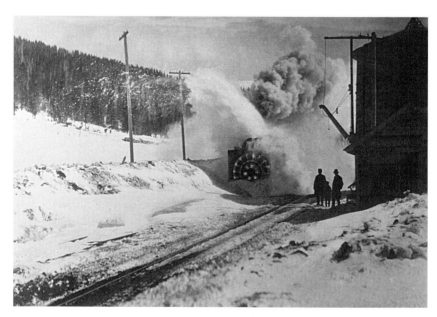

A rotary snowplow at work. (Courtesy of Scott Leslie)

of that year, he had acquired four additional marble claims from the Yule Creek White Marble Company.

The Strauss brothers were the other major quarry operators at this time. They bid a contract to use their marble on the Denver Public Library. Despite their efforts, however, the anticipated order was not to come. Amazingly, although there is little evidence that the Strauss quarry ever shipped any appreciable amount of marble, the company continued to exist until 1915, when it finally declared bankruptcy.

Colonel Meek, not unlike every other soul in the area, recognized that the completion of the railroad was vital to the success of the quarries. Unlike the rest, however, he possessed both the inclination to finish the job and the means to do so. Finally, at 3:00 P.M. on Friday, November 23, 1906, the first train pulled into Marble. It was naturally the cause for great celebration, with flags, gunshots, a band, and congratulations all around.

Though the rail lines were now available for the shipment of the blocks of marble which were being removed from the mountain, neither the Strauss brothers nor the Colorado-Yule Marble Company had yet landed a significant contract. Even so, the huge blocks of white stone were cut away from their beds and transported to the mill. Six to twelve ton blocks were hauled down the mountain on wagons in the summer. During the winter months that the quarries were able to operate, up to fifteen ton blocks could be skidded on the snow.

Despite the fact that no major orders had been received, Colonel Meek sold $3 million in stock in his company. The *Gunnison News-Champion* enthusiastically predicted a population of 5,000 to 10,000 for Marble. The town was booming. Homes and business buildings were springing up. Hotels were built and filled to overflowing, and saloons provided strong drink and other commodities to the miners and quarry workers. Electric service and telephones had arrived in town. The Colorado-Yule Marble Company was processing samples for advertising purposes, showing the quality

31

of the marble and the expertise of the craftsmen. The companies, the quarries, the town were all poised to spring into action when the orders started rolling in.

If the orders started rolling in.

CHAPTER 5

THE ORDERS ROLL IN

In October of 1907, a $500,000 order was received by Colonel Meek's company from Cuyahoga County, Ohio. They wanted Yule marble for the interior of the county court house in Cleveland. The citizens of Marble were, to say the least, ecstatic. The marble mill, already the world's largest, was expanded to a total length of 446 feet. The population of Marble grew almost overnight to 700.

Interior of the quarry - note the stairway at the right. (Courtesy of Frontier Historical Society - Shutte Collection)

Shortly thereafter, the Colorado-Yule Marble Company landed another contract for a second courthouse in Ohio. The mill was again increased in size, to 709 feet this time. A steam tractor, a huge beast of a machine, was purchased to move the marble from the quarries. The tractor sported a 110 horsepower steam engine and eight foot steel wheels.

Not all of the marble that was brought to the mill was suitable for the orders at hand, and some pieces naturally broke during cutting or carving. Many of the partially processed blocks were scattered along the Crystal River next to the railroad tracks as "rip-rap", to prevent erosion of the railbed. The larger blocks were loaded on rail cars by the mill's crane, and then dumped along the tracks just outside of Marble to make room in the mill yard. The vast majority of the white chunks are still there.

Waste marble "rip-rap" scattered along the banks of the Crystal River to ward off erosion of the river bank. (Photo by the author)

Even though the Colorado-Yule Company had built fifty furnished cottages for their employees, the two lucrative contracts required many new workers. A crude village of bunkhouses and shacks grew just to the west of the quarries. "Quarry Town" mostly housed single men. It was an unlovely little community, but it saved many of the workers the almost four mile trek from Marble each day.

Blocks of marble scattered about the site of the mill. (Courtesy of Frontier Historical Society - Shutte Collection)

The interior of the mill, showing the diamond saw at work. (Courtesy of Kjell Mitchell)

Company officials made it known to the town government that the consumption of alcohol was interfering with the efficiency and safety of the marble workers. Consequently, in December of 1908, the residents of Marble voted to make the selling of liquor illegal. They did not, however, make it illegal to purchase it. The wholesalers in Carbondale loved it, and bootleggers thrived. Many of the secluded canyons around Marble were home to illegal stills, and the production of "Rocky Mountain Spring Water" continued, law or no law.

The year of 1909 brought a labor strike which put a serious dent in the prosperity of the Colorado-Yule Company and of Marble itself. Three men were fired for refusing to work overtime with no additional compensation. In the next few days most of the work force, over 500 men, went out on strike. Unfortunately for the cause of the strikers, Meek had been paying them up to 8 dollars a day, considerably more than the wages of marble workers in other parts of the country. Even so, the strike lasted for three months, and the stockholders were beginning to express concern. Finally, in November of 1909, the union organizer suddenly left town. The strike was settled shortly thereafter, and the workers went back to the quarries and the mill. Interestingly, they went back to work at wages comparable to the national average, so the strikers accomplished somewhat less than nothing.

In 1910, with everyone back to work, Colorado-Yule obtained many contracts, including the Montana State Capitol building and the Denver Post Office. They added another 200 feet to the huge mill, and an electric tramway was constructed from the quarries to the mill. The tram replaced the steam tractor, and eased the task of transporting the tons of marble over the almost four mile trail. The grades over which the tram operated approached 17 percent in places, but it was deemed safe.

George Yule, the pioneer prospector for whom Yule Creek and the marble itself had been named, died in Rifle

Marble stored at the "marble yard" at the mill, awaiting processing. (Courtesy of Scott Leslie)

in August of 1910. In addition to serving as the first sheriff of Gunnison County, Yule had been one of the first county commissioners.

Marble was in a serious boom period. The growing little town had a grade school, a high school, and a manual training school. There were many stores, three newspapers, and as many hotels. The Marble City State Bank was opened. No saloons existed, but as mentioned, that did not appreciably slow the consumption of spirituous liquors. The population of the area was estimated at over 2,000. Marble was being advertised as being incredibly scenic, which it of course was, and as having "snowy, but not severe" winters. Since 10 feet of snow was not at all uncommon, and the railroads and wagon roads were frequently closed by snow slides, that statement might have been a trifle optimistic.

The Colorado-Yule mill was now 70 feet wide and 1,465 feet long; it stretched for over a quarter of a mile. It was fully mechanized and employed 110 men, who were processing some 40,000 cubic feet of marble a month. The

Downtown Marble - about 1907. (Courtesy of Frontier Historical Society)

contracts kept rolling in, and all seemed right with the world. This was not, unfortunately, to last. Several events conspired to spoil the optimism. A Ms. Sylvia Smith had moved to town and acquired the *Marble City Times*. She took it upon herself to launch repeated editorial attacks upon the Colorado-Yule Marble Company. This action obviously did not endear her to the good people of Marble, as Colonel Meek's company was a major player in the game to make Marble the viable, prosperous town for which they hoped. Ms. Smith did not stop at maligning Colorado-Yule for what she considered to be shady business practices. She also delighted in besmirching the reputations of many of Marble's citizens. Whether she was justified in doing so is a matter for conjecture. She obviously felt that the attacks were appropriate, for whatever reason. The townsfolk felt differently.

On March 7, 1912, David Davis was struck by a snow slide and swept over a cliff. Davis was a time-keeper for Colorado-Yule. Due to a severe snow storm, it took three days for rescue crews to reach his body. He had fallen some

The marble mill in full operation about 1915. Note the three marble fire walls protruding from the roof. At this time, the mill was over a quarter of a mile long. (Courtesy of Frontier Historical Society)

120 feet. The snow continued, depositing over three feet on the slopes of Mill Mountain, above and across the river from the Colorado-Yule processing mill. During the years of Marble's development, the slopes of Mill Mountain had been all but stripped bare of trees, in order to provide lumber for the town and for the mill itself. On the morning of March

Another photo of the mill, showing its great length. Note the rows of houses across the valley. (Courtesy of Kjell Mitchell)

21, a monstrous snow slide thundered down and across the river, crushing part of the huge mill. Interestingly, little of the snow from the avalanche actually struck the mill building. Rather, the damage was done by an almost cyclone-like wind pushed ahead of the untold tons of snow.

Fortunately, the slide struck at 6:10 in the morning, and no workers were injured. That did not stop Ms. Smith from using the tragedy as an excuse to again attack Colorado-Yule. She basically stated that "Destiny" had paid the company back for all of its "transgressions".

Enough was enough. The townspeople were incensed. Sylvia Smith was viciously, "with fiendish satisfaction", attacking the major industry of Marble. She, through her "Destiny" article, was apparently expressing great satisfaction that the company had been severely damaged and that several hundred people had been thrown out of work, albeit temporarily, by the disastrous snowslide. They held a town meeting, created and signed a petition, and invited Ms. Smith to leave Marble on a permanent basis. Some 221 of Marble's residents signed the petition. Ms. Smith naturally objected, so the authorities placed her in jail for "her own protection". The next day, they put her on a train to Carbondale, again for "her own protection".

The mill was repaired, and great effort was put forth during the following summer to insure that a slide of that proportion could not happen again. With the help of almost a ton of dynamite, thousands of posts were set into the side of Mill Mountain and interlaced with wire to hold the snow in place. In addition, a wall of waste marble blocks was started along the bank of the river. The finished wall was to be over seventy feet high and eighteen feet thick, and was to extend the entire length of the mill building.

The efforts of Colorado-Yule Marble over the next few months brought Colorado to the rank of third in marble producing states. By July, there were a million dollars worth of contracts to be filled, and Ms. Smith was nowhere to be seen. Things again looked rosy, for awhile.

Part of the waste marble that was dumped along the riverbank to prevent further damage by snowslide. (Photo by the author)

On August 10, Colonel Meek and four other employees were riding the tram down from the quarry. The brakes failed, and the tram car and its load of marble hurtled down the track. Col. Meek and the others jumped, and the Colonel suffered serious internal injuries. The others were knocked unconscious, but recovered. Channing Meek was not so lucky. He endured great pain for four days, and died on August 14, 1912. The town of Marble was plunged into what *The Marble Booster* referred to as "the Deepest Gloom". Colonel Channing Frank Meek had represented everything that the citizens of Marble had coveted for so long, and suddenly he was gone.

A month later, another tram ran out of control, eventually jumping the track and crashing into a cliff. Of the five people riding the tram, four were killed. The dead included an eight year old girl.

Mortimer Mathews was installed as the new president of Colorado-Yule. Lacking the leadership qualities of Colonel Meek, he watched the company slip into financial difficulties.

41

He went back east to secure additional backing, and was successful in obtaining almost two million dollars in loans. Marble was delighted with the news, but the additional debt seriously overextended the company.

To add to the worries, a jury in Gunnison awarded Sylvia Smith a total of about $11,000 in her suit against Colorado-Yule, the Crystal River and San Juan Railroad, and much of the citizenry of Marble. The defendants immediately appealed the decision.

The interior of the mill, showing a chunk of marble undergoing processing. (Courtesy of Kjell Mitchell)

Finally, in August of 1913, Colorado-Yule received their biggest contract, in fact, the biggest contract for any marble company as of that date. The Equitable Building of New York City required 1,200,000 square feet of marble, to the tune of a million dollars. Then, J. F. Manning took over as president and began negotiations for the contract to supply the marble for the Lincoln Memorial. The competition for the contract was worldwide. The successful bidder would enjoy a great deal of publicity and prestige, in addition to the money involved. After a visit to the Colorado-Yule quarries by a leading expert on marble, he stated that the Yule marble was the finest that he had ever seen. Buoyed by the news, the eternal optimists that apparently inhabited Marble predicted lasting prosperity for the Crystal River Valley.

On October 4, 1913, *The Marble Booster* announced that Colorado-Yule had in fact been awarded the contract for the Lincoln Memorial. Many of the other marble companies immediately raised objections, due to the fact that Colorado-Yule's bid had been the highest, by several hundred thousand dollars. Even so, the desire for the best possible quality won out, and the newspaper again exalted in the victory when the final decision was announced on January 31, 1914.

A new shop was built at the mill just to handle the Lincoln Memorial contract. In all, 36 columns were cut, each 7 feet in diameter and 46 feet high. Each column consisted of ten "drums", stacked one upon the other. The entire shipment required 40 trains of 15 cars each, 50,000 to 70,000 pounds of stone on each car. The last shipment was received in Washington months ahead of schedule. The project took over two years, and employment at the company ranged up to 1,000 workers. The population of Marble in 1913 was around 1,500.

CHAPTER 6

THE WAR YEARS

The Great War in Europe, soon to be the First World War, began in 1914. At first, the people of Marble paid the overseas activities scant attention. Work on the marble for the Lincoln Memorial was underway, and other contracts were rolling in. Marble had, after so many years of struggle and disappointment, reached its goal of prosperity. At least that was the outward appearance.

In 1914, many of the Austrian skilled workers left Marble and went back to their native country, summoned by their government. In April of 1915, Italy joined the Allied powers in World War I. Much of the population of Marble was Italian, many of whom had been hired for their stone cutting abilities. The exodus of European workers severely hurt the Colorado-Yule Company and consequently the town. More orders than ever before were pouring into the offices of the company, and there was a serious shortage of men to handle them.

To make matters worse, the United States became involved in the conflict. Not only did this action result in the induction of some of the American workers, but the marble industry was declared as non-essential to the war effort. Industries so designated found themselves unable to obtain coal, steel, or other essential materials. Construction operations, especially those that used marble, were also affected. Their orders for marble therefore dwindled, and the marble business again slowed.

There was discontent in the town of Marble itself. The Italian residents of "Dago Town" were looked upon as the lower class, and accused of various heinous crimes, such as bootlegging and gambling. The fact that many of the other good folks of Marble regularly engaged in the same activities seemed to make little difference. There were numerous fights between the two factions.

One of the mill worker's houses in Marble, about 1914. This house, as well as several others, were washed away in one of the recurring floods which plagued the town. (Courtesy of Kjell Mitchell)

The people of Marble were still trying to maintain their old optimism, believing that the present troubles were just another temporary roadblock in their quest for affluence. However, Sylvia Smith was about to rear her head once again.

The Colorado Supreme Court upheld the earlier decision against the Colorado-Yule Company and the people of Marble. Smith reappeared in Marble with the Gunnison County Sheriff in tow. The two of them strode through town, collecting shares of the damages which she had been awarded. If business owners hesitated, the Sheriff simply closed their businesses until they paid up. Some could not come up with the cash, and were forced to sell their homes or their stores to raise it. Some residents, those who worked for others, saw their wages garnisheed. Many of the defendants expressed the feeling that Colorado-Yule should bear the brunt of the payments, as they had only acted in the best interests of the company in the first place. J. F. Manning declared that he was unable to do anything because of orders from his superiors. The people of Marble had little choice but to accept his word, but hard feelings remained.

On the surface, Colorado-Yule seemed to be again prospering. The war had not slowed the demand for mausoleums or cemetery monuments, and the company was capitalizing on that fact. The orders sometimes reached $6,500 a day. The company had done a great deal of promotional work, and enjoyed an excellent reputation. Unfortunately, the prosperity of 1914 and 1915 could not outweigh the financial drain of the previous years, and they could not sell enough gravestones to overcome the otherwise dwindling demand for structural marble. The creditors of the company were demanding their interest payments, and the money was simply not there. Despite the outward enthusiasm, the company and the town were poised on the brink of a long slide downward.

It began to snow heavily on the day after Christmas of 1915, and snowed almost continuously until January 16, 1916. There was no way to get to the quarry, and even the snowplows were snowbound. The mill workers were able to work inside of the mill, but they shortly ran out of the normal fresh supply of marble. It was almost February before the tracks and the roads were cleared enough to use. After the destructive snow slide of 1912, the marble retaining wall had been built to prevent further damage to the mill. The wall proved its worth after the huge storm, but it was obvious that any further slides would ride up over the accumulated snow and the wall, so the mill was closed again for a short while.

The company carried the appearance of financial health into the first months of 1916. The Colorado-Yule Company ranked just behind the Italian Carrara marble works in size. However, the company was some $3,500,000 in debt, and the wolves were approaching the door. Unable to meet its interest obligations, the seemingly solvent company was placed in receivership in July of 1916. Efforts to save the company failed, and operations ceased entirely in April of 1917.

To add to the woes of the little town, a fire swept through the center of Marble on August 24, 1916. The fire broke out early in the morning in the back of the drug store and quickly spread to surrounding buildings. One downtown structure, the Swigart Building, was purposely blown up with thirty-five sticks of dynamite. That helped to stop the advance of the fire, and it was brought under control. The blaze destroyed 6 buildings, spelling financial ruin for most of their owners. The majority of the buildings were under insured. However, one of the owners had heavily insured his building, and there was suspicion that he had set the fire.

With the quarries and the mill closed, an understandable gloom fell over the town. Even so, there was a reluctance on the part of the now unemployed marble workers to leave. To quote the *Marble Booster*, "We expect the marble mills to reopen for business bigger and better than ever, before many months. There is too much money invested and too much fine marble in the quarry for them to be idle for long. We believe the town of Marble has yet to see its most prosperous year." On August 26, 1916, the headline proclaimed: "Brighter Days for Marble Are in Sight. The End of Our Troubles is Nearing. So, CHEER UP!"

The winter of 1916-1917 had been another severe one, and the resulting runoff the following June took out the railroad in several places between Marble and Redstone, as well as the bridge on Main Street in Marble. Damage was also heavy along both Carbonate Creek and the Crystal River.

In October, the Crystal River and San Juan Railroad ceased operations into Marble. The editor of the *Marble Booster*, the newspaper that had so recently expressed confidence that the "company" would soon be back in business, moved to Kansas. He was not alone in leaving town. Several of the merchants closed their stores and departed, a few of them still expressing the now dimming hope that the quarries would reopen. The exodus of residents continued, as the approaching winter of 1917-1918 would find Marble without train or telephone service, and with no doctor.

CHAPTER 7

THE TWENTIES - STILL STRUGGLING TO STAY ALIVE

The assets of the Colorado-Yule Marble Company, including the mill, the railroad, the quarries, and the land and buildings in and around Marble, had been split into three parcels for the sheriff's sale in 1919. It was hoped that one entity would purchase all three parcels, thus keeping the operation together. This did not happen. However, the separate owners expressed an interest in reopening the quarries and the mill, so the 81 people remaining in Marble were naturally optimistic.

Legal battles stretched into April of 1921, when the Colorado Supreme Court finally cleared the way for the new owners to pay the back taxes and begin operations. There was much celebrating at the news.

The Yule Marble Company of Colorado was formed by the new owners of the railroad and the mill. The successful bidders for the quarries and the tram line then began work as the Carrara Yule Company. Both companies spent much of 1921 in repairing their respective holdings.

Meanwhile, a third company, the Colorado White Marble Company, was formed by the Mormon church of Missouri. They planned to reopen the old Strauss quarries and secure enough marble to build a new tabernacle in Independence, Missouri. The plan was to drive a tunnel some 1200 feet into White House Mountain. The tunnel was to be large enough to accommodate a locomotive, so that the removed marble could be loaded directly onto the train cars. They labored for several years on the project, succeeding in tunneling 450 feet into the mountain, but they went into receivership in 1926. No marble was ever removed by the company.

Also in 1921, news of a rich silver trace brought would-be prospectors to the area of Carbonate Creek, but little silver was found. The hopes of the populace still rested on the marble deposits.

In early 1922, the Denver and Rio Grande Railroad agreed to repair the old Crystal River and San Juan line. In return, they were guaranteed annual shipments of 1,500 carloads of marble. The two new companies were receiving orders for marble, and the population began to swell once more; by July, it was up to around 400. Yule Marble and Carrara agreed to combine operations, rather than compete against each other. The employment force grew to around 200, even though only $12,000 worth of marble was shipped during 1922. However, the train pulled into town in July for the first time in five years, and enthusiasm was again high. All was not good fortune, however. A portion of the mill roof collapsed under snow load in December, injuring two of the workers. Also, in early 1923 two federal marshals confiscated two stills and a large quantity of illegal liquor. Two men were arrested, and several others were nowhere to be found. According to the *Gunnison News-Champion*, "As a result of the raid, the retail price of hooch advanced perceptibly. . ."

William Woods, one of the founders of Marble, died at the age of eighty-two in April of 1923. He was mourned by the entire town, and his body was shipped to Illinois for burial.

Transportation to and from Marble had not improved considerably. The railroad was running, but the wagon road down toward Redstone and Carbondale was still subject to rock and snow slides. Between rocks and holes and mud, the citizens described the road as "Hell".

The remainder of 1923 was relatively uneventful, save for a fire in May that burned several downtown buildings, and the occasional runaway marble tram car. The year closed with a population near 500 and numerous marble contracts from Chicago, Detroit, and the Pacific Coast.

The duplication of efforts involved in operating the two companies side by side proved cumbersome, so they agreed in July of 1924 to merge into a new company, to be called the Consolidated Yule Marble Company. The total shipments of marble for 1923 and 1924 exceeded $570,000.

In November of 1924, a J. B. Jones, president of a Tennessee marble company, leased the Consolidated property for a year, with an option to buy it. The result was the Tennessee-Colorado Marble Company. Jones announced that there was nothing in the world that would halt production of the Yule Creek marble. He was, it turned out, a bit too optimistic.

On April 22, 1925, a huge fire destroyed about one-third of the mill. It was fed by some forty barrels of oil that had been stored in a part of the mill. There was some talk that the fire may have been set by arsonists, outside interests who were attempting to unionize the mill at that time. As luck, (or design), would have it, the water supply was undergoing repairs, so there was little remaining pressure. The townspeople watched helplessly as the enormous building went up in flames. The building was insured for $195,000, however, total damages were assessed as $531,000, which put a serious dent in the financial health of the company. J. B. Jones announced that he was pulling out, and relinquished his lease. The Consolidated Company tried to continue operations, but was forced to close temporarily in August. They did reopen, however, and continued to operate during the rest of 1925 and 1926. In addition, the White Marble Company and the Colorado Marble Company continued operations, unaffected by the fire.

Although production was slow during 1927, a Jacob Smith purchased the Consolidated property for a million dollars. Smith had been active in the Colorado Marble Company, and his actions buoyed the spirits of the populace. One major contract, for the Huntington Memorial in Pasadena, California, was completed in 1928. In November, Smith sold half of his interest to the Vermont Marble Company, who then formed the Yule Colorado Company. As 1929 began, the old optimism reappeared. Prosperity, it seemed, was just around the corner.

To add to the hopefulness of the residents, two latter-day prospectors discovered what looked like a rich vein of gold between Marble and Crystal. Subsequent mining activities resulted in another strike nearby, and excitement was rampant. The gold deposits never resulted in the hoped for bonanza, but they did help to publicize the Marble area.

On October 24, 1929, "Black Thursday", the stock market crashed, plunging the entire country into an economic depression that was to last most of the next ten years. Marble was of course effected, since the building, mining, and transportation trades all slowed. Even so, the Vermont Marble Company was making daily shipments, and seemed close to closing a deal to supply marble for the new Customs Building in Denver. Some activity in lead, silver, and gold mining continued, and it was felt that there was still every reason for enthusiasm.

CHAPTER 8

THE TOMB OF THE UNKNOWN SOLDIER

As if in validation of the seemingly ceaseless optimism which pervaded the citizens of Marble, 1930 saw the awarding of a contract that was to be considered the most prestigious in the history of marble production in the United States. Due to the quality of the Yule Creek marble and the size of the Yule Colorado quarry, the company was contracted to provide the huge block of marble necessary for the construction of the Tomb of the Unknown Soldier at Arlington National Cemetery, in Arlington, Virginia.

After more than a year of work by seventy-five men, the gigantic block was at last freed from its bed. It initially weighed some 124 tons, making it the largest block of marble ever quarried. A special wire saw was installed in the bowels of the quarry to trim it to its shipping dimensions. The rough measurements were to be 14 feet by 7.4 feet by 6 feet. Even after trimming, the block weighed 56 tons.

An enormous derrick had been shipped from Vermont just to lift the massive block out of the quarry. The section of the quarry which held the block was some 125 feet deep, and the only way out was through the roof. The derrick had been reinforced and specially rigged to take the weight, but it was still an agonizingly tense time for the workers. The massive chunk of marble was hoisted a few inches off the floor of the quarry, and held there for 15 minutes while a final check of the stress points of the crane were checked. The hoist held, and the huge block slowly emerged into the sunlight.

It was lowered to a specially built railroad car which was supported on one end by small mine car wheels and on the other by an oak beam. The contraption was then attached to two electric locomotives to be skidded down the 3.9 mile track to Marble. That trip alone took four days, including stops for photos and one day to repair the brakes on the lead locomotive. After the block was crated and braced for shipment, under the watchful eyes of 24-hour guards, it began its journey down the valley on its way to Vermont for cutting, and then on to Arlington Cemetery for installation. The years of 1932 and 1933 were slow in Marble, the effects of the national depression weakening most segments of the American economy. The building trades were extremely dormant, especially the type of construction that would consider marble. In March of 1932, word reached the residents of Marble that their old nemesis, Sylvia Smith, had died in Denver. There was little mourning of her passing by the 150 or so citizens of the little mountain town.

In 1933, the current rumor was that the Yule Colorado Company was to be picked to supply the marble for the new Federal Office Building in Denver. There was some activity in the quarries and the mill, mostly repairs to ready the operations for production. Then, the architects of the United States Customs House Annex, also in Denver, indicated that they intended to use Yule marble. Despite attempts by Georgia marble operations to underbid Yule Colorado, the $107,000 contract was awarded to the Colorado company. The company was also shipping some headstones and mausoleums, so the little town limped through the mid-30's.

The winter of 1936-1937 brought a particularly vicious blizzard, leaving the town snowbound and without lights. Spring finally arrived, but then July brought very heavy rain, sending Carbonate Creek over its banks. The resultant flood and mudslides damaged or destroyed bridges and buildings, causing several thousand dollars worth of damage.

In the late 30's, the rest of the nation was beginning to flirt with prosperity for the first time since the crash of 1929. With increases in income came an interest in tourism. Roads throughout Colorado were undergoing improvement, and automotive travel was just beginning on any kind of a serious level. The scenic beauty of the Crystal River Valley began to attract, for the first time, those who were not interested in either marble or precious metals. A ski hill was opened east of town in 1939, drawing crowds from Redstone, Carbondale, and Glenwood Springs.

Marble production was still sporadic, and slowed even more with the outbreak of World War II. Again, the marble industry was declared nonessential to national defense. The quarries closed for the winter of 1940, with some question whether they would ever again open. Many families left town for the winter, as they had done for years; this time there was no assurance that they would be back.

The quarries did reopen in June of 1941, but, possibly for the first time, the old optimism had dimmed. As 1941 wore on, more people left town, never to return.

CHAPTER 9

THE FORTIES - NO GOOD NEWS

The year of 1941 brought with it an uncharacteristic lack of optimism. The residents of the Marble, for perhaps the first time, were facing the likelihood that the mill and the quarries were on the verge of closing, maybe forever. Families continued to leave town in the face of the rumors.

On August 8, 1941, blue skies gave way to towering thunderheads as a summer storm swept the hills above Marble. At a little after 3:00 in the afternoon, the brown wall of a flash flood raced down Carbonate Creek and hit Marble. The tons of water, mud, and rocks tore through the town, damaging the water system, moving and destroying buildings. It left a one thousand foot path of devastation through the middle of town, with rocks, mud, and uprooted trees piling up to a height of twenty feet. Fortunately, the flood missed the mill. Even more fortunately, there was no loss of life.

Then, on September 11, the Vermont Marble Company made the announcement that the workers and residents had been dreading; operations were to cease on or about December 1. The Crystal River and San Juan Railroad had been trying to close the line for some time, and immediately petitioned the Interstate Commerce Commission to do just that. Uncharacteristically, there was none of the usual hopefulness which had permeated the populace of the little valley. There was, for the first time, talk of Marble becoming a ghost town.

When the end came, it came gradually. On October 25, 1941, the quarry shut down and the last blocks of marble came slowly down the steep grades of the tram line. Then, on November 15, two weeks prior to the predicted date, the world's largest Marble mill shut its doors for the last time.

As if to emphasize the finality of the closing, the next few months saw not only the removal of the tracks of the

Remains of a building after the 1945 flood. (Courtesy of Frontier Historical Society - Shutte Collection)

Crystal River and San Juan Railroad, but also the dismantling and shipping of much of the machinery which had transported and processed the marble for so long. More of the residents left along with the machinery, but a few stubborn inhabitants refused to abandon the Crystal River Valley, the Town of Marble.

The year of 1942 was very slow in Marble. Only a drug store, a barber shop, and the post office were still open. The United States was at war with Japan by that time, and the remaining townsfolk settled into the quiet life of an isolated mountain town. A few of the old lead and silver mines reopened during 1943, and the population was fifty or so. The post office which had been the object of such hope half a century before was closed during 1943, and many of the employee houses which had been built by Colorado Yule were moved to Grand Junction. After the last of the milling machinery and the buildings had been shipped out, the train made one last slow trip down the Crystal River Valley, taking up the tracks behind it as it went.

On July 31, 1945, another flash flood hit Marble like a fist. It was, by all reports, far worse than the one in 1941. A thirty to forty foot wall of mud, rocks, and water swept down Carbonate Creek, damaging almost all of the buildings left in town. Remarkably, the population of about forty escaped with only a few injuries. The same storms buried the roads on both sides of Marble, cutting off access to Redstone down the valley, and sending some twenty-one rock and mud slides across the road up to Crystal.

Overview of Marble during the 1945 flood. (Courtesy of Frontier Historical Society - Shutte Collection)

As the 40s ended, there was still a faint glimmer of hope that the quarries might reopen, given a post-war demand for construction marble or improvements to the roads down the valley toward Carbondale. Neither of these events occurred, however, and 1950 arrived quietly in Marble. The population continued to dwindle. At one time, only Charles and Marjorie Orlosky and Theresa Herman remained in Marble. Then, the Orloskys moved to the other side of Beaver Lake, outside of the town limits. This left Ms. Herman.

All that remained of the great marble mill after the machinery was removed and the remainder of the wooden walls were demolished. Note the still-standing marble fire walls and some of the marble columns. (Courtesy of Frontier Historical Society - Shutte Collection)

Sentinels guarding the memories of the marble mill. (Photo by the author)

Though the town somehow continued to resist becoming an actual ghost town, this was quite a change from the population of almost 2,000 in the early years of the century. The Vermont Marble Company failed to pay the county taxes on their land holdings. A Carbondale sheepman named Elmer Bair, who had been leasing those lands for sheep grazing for several years, purchased many of the claims.

One of the very few remaining buildings at the mill site. (Photo by the author)

In 1953, the Basic Chemical Company was formed. The aim of the new enterprise was to process and sell the limestone from which the Yule Creek Marble was made. Crushed limestone was in demand for everything from toothpaste to roofing material; Colorado alone used in excess of 28,000 tons per year. The company purchased 1,600 acres from Elmer Bair, and set up processing equipment and a kiln in Glenwood Springs. The principles in the company approached the Gunnison County Commissioners, asking that the road to Carbondale be improved. The company did succeed in hauling away a great deal of the 80,000 tons of scrap marble at the old mill site, including most of the massive retaining wall which had been built next to the river as protection against snow slides. However, the road improvements were not forthcoming, and transportation expenses forced Basic Chemical to abandon their plans to continue. Once again, the remote location of Marble doomed the plans to exploit the riches that lay in the surrounding hills.

The remainder of 1955 brought a lead and silver strike at the Little Darling Mine three miles from Marble, the completion of an airstrip, and the construction of Beaver Lake Lodge. Tourism was beginning to multiply the population during the summer months; hiking, horseback riding, fishing, and the relatively new sport of "jeeping", negotiating the primitive mountain roads in four wheel drive vehicles, were bringing in the tourists. However, some of the winters found only twenty or so determined souls sticking it out.

The 1950's also saw increasing use of the old St. Paul Episcopal Church. The building had originally been brought from Aspen in 1908, and had been closed in 1941. Ambrose and John Williams, two Marble pioneers, held summer services for some years. In 1952 Kareen and Raquel Loudermilk began holding prayer meetings. Eventually, the congregation of the Community Church attempted to take over the church building. The Episcopal Bishop resisted the efforts, and eventually reclaimed their church. Services are still held each Sunday during the summer months.

The St. Paul Episcopal Church, moved from Aspen in 1908, and still in use. (Courtesy of Frontier Historical Society - Shutte Collection)

THE MARBLE SKI AREA

Although the Vermont Marble Company made several moves during 1963 which indicated an interest in the possibility of reopening the quarries to which they had retained possession, little was to come of it. The quarries that had represented the hopes of the Marble populace for so long remained deserted. The huge holes that had been blasted and cut into the Treasure Mountain Dome were silent, slowly filling with snow-melt water. If Marble were to recover any of its former activity, it appeared that the town would have to look elsewhere.

The Oberlander Corporation of Denver purchased 1,500 acres around Marble in 1964, announcing intentions of developing a ski area and summer resort northeast of town. Downhill skiing was gaining a great deal of popularity at that time. The ski areas at Aspen were attracting the attention of increasing numbers of winter tourists. The town of Vail was in its infancy, but it was on its way to becoming one of the world's largest ski areas. Marble was, admittedly, somewhat isolated, for all intents at the "end of the road". Of course, the same could be said of Crested Butte, another fledgling ski town on the other side of Schofield Pass. Also, Aspen was reduced to one access route every winter when Independence Pass was closed.

Marble was, it was reasoned, "blessed" with an abundance of snow every winter. In fact, as any resident would verify, the snows came as early as September and stayed late into the spring. Marble seemed to possess the requisite ingredients for a snow oriented destination resort. The snow was certainly there, as was the elevation and the exquisite scenery. If Marble could in fact develop interest in such a resort, maybe the area could finally regain some of the prosperity that it had enjoyed in the early part of the 20th century, and which it had sought to recapture for so long.

However, as had been the case for so many years, prosperity continued to elude the people of Marble. No one reason can be singled out for the failure of the grandiose plans. Rather, it was a combination of things that doomed them. Marble was in fact secluded. That fact alone had historically hurt the marble industry, the difficulty of transporting the weighty blocks of stone making Yule marble less than competitive in the world market. In addition, the steep slopes that generated snow and mud slides in the early days still made travel up the Crystal River Valley chancy at times. Also, unlike Aspen, Marble had no commercial airport, only a 5,000 foot unpaved airstrip.

The proposed ski area was located on a west-facing slope, so the afternoon sun caused rapid deterioration of the snow conditions. There was also opposition to their plan to cut ski runs through virgin forest on Arkansas Mountain.

The developers of the Marble ski area lacked the funds necessary to construct a world-class ski resort. The resorts that were being developed at that time, the Aspens and the Vails of Colorado, the Snowbirds of Utah, did have the requisite deep pockets to both build the huge, multi-lift areas and to publicize them to the world's growing ski market. Even if the Marble ski area would have become a reality, there is some doubt that it could have competed with the myriad other Rocky Mountain ski resorts.

The deep snows have attracted the cross-country skier, the snowmobiler, and the snowshoe enthusiast. The spectacular scenery, abundant wildlife, and the very solitude that served to doom the more ambitious projects in the Marble area have attracted the more adventurous of the tourists. Throughout the 70's and most of the 80's, Marble was to remain quiet. It was the year-round home to a few hardy souls, the summer home to others, and the destination for hikers, campers, four-wheelers, fishermen, and photographers.

CHAPTER 10

THE QUARRY REOPENS!

The quarry remained closed for some 49 years. Had it not been for the dream of a University of Colorado graduate named Stacy Dunn, it might still be closed.

In 1988, Dunn was working in the petroleum industry. As he checked oil wells southwest of Aspen, he happened upon the long-dormant quarry on the mountain above Marble. Envisioning the reopening of the quarry, he instilled his excitement in his wife, Linda, and Greg Faith, who was to become his business partner. They talked to the Vermont Marble Company, who still owned the quarry site. The new company, to be called Colorado Yule Marble Company, acquired a 70 year lease from Vermont Marble. With the financial backing of Hambro Bank in London, England, they set about to reactivate the quarry.

Unfortunately, only a year after putting his dream into motion, Stacy Dunn was killed in an auto accident. He was on his way to Gunnison to obtain a permit for the operation of the quarry when the crash ended his life. He was 35 years old. A new bridge over the Crystal River was named the Stacy Dunn Memorial Bridge in his honor. A plaque with his name and his image is set into a block of marble at the bridge. The legend below his face reads, "Vision with Integrity".

Linda Dunn, an Evergreen schoolteacher, carried on Stacy's vision. She sat on the board of directors of Colorado Yule, providing a continuation of the dream, of her late husband's love of the stone. Her apprehension about the reputation of the company and of the quarry was balanced against the bottom line concerns of the London bankers.

In September of 1990, the first block of marble to be removed from the quarry in 49 years was hauled slowly down the four mile road to Marble. It weighed 22 tons and, fittingly, it crossed the river on the Stacy Dunn Memorial Bridge.

The monument to Stacy Dunn in Marble. Before his death, he was instrumental in the reopening of the marble quarries. (Photo by the author)

For a period of time, the rail yard at Glenwood Springs contained a stockpile of the huge blocks of marble from Colorado Yule's quarry. About 100 tons of the sparkling white rock were shipped every two months, bound for Italy and Japan, or to be made into headstones for the graves of American veterans. Marble from the new operation was used in the renovation of Denver's Courthouse, and at Denver International Airport.

Another principal in the reactivation of the quarry was also killed in an auto accident. Ferdinando Borghetti, an internationally known expert in marble deposits, was initially hired as quarry master. He exhibited considerable enthusiasm about the Treasure Mountain marble deposits, and was of a great deal of assistance in determining the direction in which to extend the quarry operations. He was killed when he attempted to avoid hitting a deer on Highway 133, and his car went into the Crystal River.

Not long after the reopening of the quarry, an opportunity arose to provide the marble for a new monument at Arlington National Cemetery. It was to be a commemorative monument to female military veterans. The chance to vie for the honor of providing the required pure white marble for the Women in Military Service for America Memorial was looked upon as a opportunity to regain some of the earlier glory of Marble. The monument would rest near the Tomb of the Unknown Soldier in Arlington, for which the quarry provided the stone many years previously.

Unfortunately, the provided sample was too soft to be used, and the other marble available at that time was crossed by darker veins, considered unsuitable for the monument. Ultimately, marble from the state of Vermont was chosen. Even so, Colorado Yule decided to donate a block of marble to the project. The donated stone was a "sister slab" to the block which had been cut free from the mountain over 50 years previously for the Tomb of the Unknown Soldier. It had been sitting in the quarry for all of those years, and it was felt that it should be used for something special. It will be placed at the end of the hall of honor for the new memorial.

The management of Colorado Yule was intent on locating and quarrying more of the pure white marble that gave the area its reputation in the early part of the 20th century. Many marble quarries, including the famous Carrara Marble operation in Italy, are open pit mines, not unlike strip mines. Due to the surrounding mountainous terrain and the severe slope of the marble beds, the Marble quarry more closely resembles a mine. Tunnels have been driven in several directions, in search of quality stone.

The quarry is a cold place, sitting at over 9,300 feet in elevation. Snowmelt seeps into the bowels of the "mine", and combines with the water used to cool the 13-foot cutting blades and the resultant marble dust to form a white slurry on the floor. During much of the year it freezes, creating treacherous footing for the quarry workers. After the top, side, and bottom cuts have been made on a fresh block, a flat metal "bag" is slipped under it and inflated with water until the block of marble breaks away from the wall. A diamond-impregnated wire saw is used to cut the blocks to the required sizes for shipping.

A few of the coal miners, who lost their jobs when the Mid-Continent mine closed, found employment with Colorado Yule. The work in the marble quarry is both slower and safer than coal mining. While there is little danger of collapse, inhalation of dust, or explosion, the quarry produced in a year the approximate tonnage that could be removed from a coal mine in a day.

The old quarry road was improved by the new company. The roadway, originally the pathway of the electric trolley, was widened and improved to accommodate the huge trucks which were used to haul the marble blocks down the mountain.

Then, as had happened so many times in the past, things began to go sour. The demand for marble decreased, and Colorado Yule found itself in financial difficulty. Once again, the big quarry closed.

Rex Loesby had been an engineer for Colorado Yule, but he left the company in 1991. After the former company went into foreclosure, Loesby began making moves to acquire

A 30-ton marble block at sculptor Greg Tonozzi's studio, awaiting transformation. (Photo by the author)

control of the quarry. He picked up the existing lease for the property, bought various of the notes payable by the old company, and acquired many of the assets through the foreclosure proceedings. The quarry was put back into operation in August, 1999 by Sierra Minerals Corporation, of which Rex Loesby is President.

Marble, especially the pure white stone produced by the Colorado quarries and by Carrara in Italy, has long been prized by sculptors. Michelangelo used Carrara marble for many of his magnificent works. Modern sculptors such as Greg Tonozzi of New Castle covet the snowy fine-grained stone. Until the reactivation of the quarry, the only marble available locally was from the discards

The Crystal Mill - located on the Crystal river between Marble and Crystal City. The mill was built in 1893. (Courtesy of Frontier Historical Society - Shutte Collection)

Site of the MARBLE/marble symposium, held annually near the site of the old marble mill. (Photo by the author)

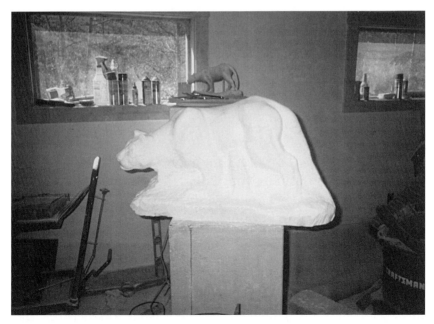

A work in progress in the studio of Jack Orlosky of Marble. (Photo by the author)

"To the Dancers Belong the Universe" - by Greg Tonozzi. On display at 23rd and Grand Avenue, Glenwood Springs, Colorado. (Photo by the author)

of earlier years. Tonozzi has been instrumental in the formation of an annual event called the Marble/marble Symposium. It is a gathering of sculptors and would-be sculptors in an aspen glen not far from the old mill site.

As the 20th century ends, the little town of Marble has settled into the life of an isolated Rocky Mountain town. The year-round population is made up of retirees, a few hardy commuters, and the owners and employees of the few businesses left in town. However, its sheer isolation dictates that it will be sought out by those seeking solace from their normal workaday world. It has become a haven for the tourist. They are lured by the magnificent scenery, by the fish in Beaver Lake, by the opportunity to walk among the massive marble columns that once helped to support the world's largest marble mill. Some pass on through Marble on their way to the four-wheel drive road which leads on up to the much-photographed Crystal Mill and to Crystal City and beyond.

The foundation of the Catholic church, made of marble. The church was never finished. (Courtesy of Frontier Historical Society - Shutte Collection)

There are chunks of marble everywhere. They can be seen on the banks of the Crystal River between Carbondale and Redstone, and again above Redstone on the road to Marble. As the traveler approaches Marble, huge white shapes are visible through the trees. In town, the RV park

Wine racks? Marble honey combs? Part of the leavings from the mill. (Photo by the author)

The mill site today. Note the remaining columns which at one time supported the walls and the overhead crane, and the remaining fire wall. (Courtesy of Frontier Historical Society - Shutte Collection)

is filled with whimsical shapes left over from long-ago marble processing, and the marble foundation of the Catholic Church which was never finished gleams whitely through the bushes. At the site of the mill itself, the area is littered with odd shaped pieces ranging from a few pounds to a few tons in weight. It looks as though a race of giants was interrupted during a strange game of some kind, and they threw down their gaming pieces in disgust.

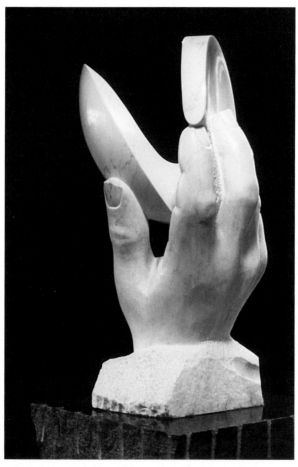

"The Spirit of Healing" - Yule marble sculpture by Greg Tonozzi. The sculpture is on display in the lobby of Valley View Hospital, Glenwood Springs, Colorado. (Courtesy of Greg Tonozzi)

A PARTIAL LIST OF BUILDINGS CONSTRUCTED
WITH THE USE OF YULE MARBLE

ARIZONA:
Kingman .... Mojave County Court House
Phoenix .... Adams Hotel

CALIFORNIA:
Los Angeles .... Merritt Building
Los Angeles .... Athletic Club
Los Angeles .... Citizen's National Bank
Los Angeles .... Merchants National Bank
Los Angeles .... Examiner Building
Pasadena .... Huntington Mausoleum
Pasadena .... Post Office
San Francisco .... Sun-Treasury Building
San Francisco .... City Hall

COLORADO:
Denver .... Old Court House
Denver .... New Court House
Denver .... State Capitol
Denver .... State Capitol Annex
Denver .... City & County Building
Denver .... Cheeseman Memorial
Denver .... Post Office
Denver .... Colorado National Bank
Denver .... Broadway Bank
Denver .... Union Station
Denver .... Metropolitan Building
Denver .... Barth Mausoleum
Denver .... Daniel & Fisher Building
Denver .... Colorado State Museum
Denver .... Immaculate Conception Cathedral
Greeley .... Post Office

DISTRICT OF COLUMBIA:
Washington .... Lincoln Memorial

IDAHO:
Pocatello .... Post Office

ILLINOIS:
Chicago .... Telephone Building
Chicago .... Rosehill Mausoleum

INDIANA:
Evansville .... Citizen's National Bank

IOWA:
Plover .... Lind Mausoleum

MASSACHUSETTS:
Cambridge .... Wiedener Memorial

MINNESOTA:
Minneapolis .... McKnight Building

MISSOURI:
St. Louis .... German-American Institute
Kansas City .... Chambers Estate Building

MONTANA:
Billings .... Montana Power House
Helena .... State Capitol Building

NEBRASKA:
St. Paul .... Howard County Court House
Greeley .... Court House
Omaha .... West Lawn Mausoleum
Omaha .... Brandeis Subway
Omaha .... Union Pacific Building
Omaha .... Douglas County Court House

Lincoln .... Lincoln High School
Lincoln .... Bancroft High School
Lincoln .... First National Bank
Lincoln .... Chapin Building
Broken Arrow .... IOOF Building
Sidney .... First National Exchange Bank

NEW YORK:
New York .... Equitable Building

OHIO:
Cleveland .... Cuyahoga County Court House
Cleveland .... City Hall
Youngstown .... Court House

OKLAHOMA:
Tulsa .... Tulsa High School

OREGON:
Portland .... First National Bank

TEXAS:
Houston.................... Union National Bank

VIRGINIA:
Arlington................. Tomb of the Unknown Soldier

CHAPTER 1

THE "GRAND HOGBACK"

Between the Central Rockies to the east and the high, flat reaches of the Colorado Plateau to the west lies a massive formation known as the Grand Hogback. It begins in the vicinity of Chair Mountain, southwest of the town of Marble, and runs north and west to Meeker. It lies to the west of Redstone, Carbondale, and Glenwood Springs, and passes under the Colorado River near New Castle. The layers of rocks in the Hogback laid flat in the distant past, but they are now almost vertical in places. Sedimentary layers, which were laid down over a span of several million years, were cracked and pushed up by the forces that formed the Rockies.

The "Grand Hogback" - a coal-bearing geological formation which runs from Chair Mountain above Marble to near Meeker. (Photo by the author)

The Hogback exhibits a miles long spine of harder rocks, mostly Mesaverde and Dakota sandstones. This ridge is resistant to erosion by wind, water, and the freezing/thawing cycles of the Colorado high country. This spine has protected the other, softer layers of sedimentary rock. Some of these layers contain seams of coal, varying from a few inches to several feet in thickness. The size of the seams and the grade of the coal depends on several factors.

In the late Cretaceous Period of prehistory, much of the area which was to become western Colorado was covered by a shallow sea. At the edges of that sea were enormous swamps, somewhat similar to the Florida Everglades of today. Over millions of years, the vegetation and the animal residents of the swamps died, adding to a soft, spongy layer of rotting organic material. Over time, much of this material decayed completely, providing nutrients for future generations of growth. The residue gradually built in thickness, creating a closely packed layer. This layer, of course, varied greatly in depth, depending on the type of material involved and the period of existence of the swamp itself.

As changing climactic conditions or physical uplift of the area brought about the end of the swamps, the remaining material was covered by deposition of new sediments, the sands carried by runoff from higher areas. The resultant layers of sandstone or other sedimentary rock sealed the organic material off from the air, creating the necessary anaerobic (without oxygen) conditions for its transformation into a material known as peat. Given the increased pressure of added layers of rock above it and the heat generated by that pressure and by volcanic activity, the peat was gradually compressed, changing the molecular structure into that of coal.

There are several grades of coal. Lignite is brownish-black, sort of a cross between peat and coal. It is the least valuable of the grades, giving off much less heat than the higher grades when burned. Bituminous, or "soft" coal, is the most plentiful. There are grades within the bituminous classification, some of which were used for home heating and railroad engines, while others were suitable for "coking", heating under low oxygen conditions to produce coke, a fuel used in metallurgical processing. Harder still, but somewhat more scarce, is anthracite coal. If coal is subjected to enough heat and pressure, it ultimately forms graphite. The coal deposits of the Grand Hogback run the gambit from lignite to anthracite, but are mostly bituminous. The heat which contributed to the formation of the coal seams came both from pressure and from "laccoliths". These geological events were the result of magma, the melted rock deep in the earth, pushing up through cracks or vents in the rock. If the magma breaks through into the open air, it is called lava. If it does not, the pressure of the molten rock tends to push up the overlaying layers of rock. Both Mount Sopris near Carbondale and Chair Mountain above Marble are the result of laccolith activity.

Another product of the decomposition of plant material is marsh gas, known as methane. It is poisonous, but it is most feared by miners because it is quite explosive. Early coal miners called it "fire damp". The heat from the laccoliths of Chair Mountain and Mount Sopris produced excessive amounts of methane, and since early coal mining relied on the use of both torches and explosives, the pockets of methane trapped in the coal resulted in numerous deadly explosions and fires.

The threat of methane is not the only danger faced by coal miners. Because of the uplift which formed the Grand Hogback, the coal seams tend to lay at rather severe angles within the surrounding rock. A highway grade of 7 percent is considered steep, calling for gearing down and the use of brakes on vehicles. Most of the coal deposits in the Hogback lie at angles between 12 degrees and 45 degrees, increasing the difficulty and the danger of working in the mines. Also, the coal seams are subject to "faulting". Faulting results from the fracturing and shifting of the rock layers, displacing the layer of coal within the mountain. Some of these shifts have raised or lowered a portion of a seam many feet, necessitating a search through solid rock to locate the continuation of a coal deposit.

Even with the inherent dangers of mining coal on the western slope of the Rockies, the quality and apparent quantity of the fuel source drew the imaginations and the energies of a special breed of entrepreneur.

CHAPTER 2

JOHN CLEVELAND OSGOOD - AN AMERICAN ARISTOCRAT

The story of the early days of Redstone, Colorado is very much the story of John Cleveland Osgood. Osgood was, during the last few years of the 1800's and the first part of the 20th century, a promoter, an industrialist, and one of the richest men of the time. He was also the architect of one of the great social experiments of that era.

In the late 1800's and the early 1900's, there existed a breed of man that could be described as "The American Aristocracy". These were men of great power, great influence, great wealth. They were, almost invariably, ambitious, single-minded, and ruthless. Possessed of giant egos, they ran their companies and controlled their employees with iron hands. It was not unusual for them to also control local and state authorities, sheriffs, judges and the like, when it was advantageous to do so. They have been referred to as "barons" or "empire builders," and thought of themselves as monarchs, presiding over their "monarchies" very much like European kings had done for centuries. These "barons' made their own rules, and in most cases, theirs was the final word. John Cleveland Osgood was to rise from humble beginnings to become one of these men.

John Osgood was born in Brooklyn, New York on March 6, 1851. His father was Samuel Warburton Osgood, his mother Mary Hill Cleveland Osgood. Members of his family originally came from England, and founded Cleveland, Ohio and Andover, Massachusetts. By the time he was eight years old, he had been left an orphan. After a few years of living with Quaker relatives and attending the Friends Boarding School in Providence, Rhode Island, he quit school at the age of fourteen and entered the world of business. His first job was as an office boy at a Rhode Island cotton mill for a reported wage of $1.50 a month. After about two years, he

John Cleveland Osgood, American aristocrat, social architect, and "Fuel King of the West." (Courtesy of Frontier Historical Society)

went to work for the William H. Ladd Produce Company. At that time, he enrolled in the Peter Cooper Institute, known then as the "Poor Man's Harvard", and majored in accounting. The Cooper Institute became famous for graduating future leaders of industry.

Osgood has been described as a short but handsome man, with wide set eyes and a broad forehead. He was immaculate in dress, somewhat of a perfectionist, and a shrewd negotiator.

After graduation from the Peter Cooper Institute, at the age of 19, Osgood went to work for the Union Mining Company in Ottumwa, Iowa, as a bookkeeper. Later, at age 23, he became the cashier of the First National Bank of Burlington. While there, he became aware of the high rates of earnings of coal companies. In those days, coal was the primary energy source, used for industry, for transportation, for home heating. Leaving the bank in 1876, he acquired controlling interest in an enterprise known as the White Breast Coal Company, which was a major supplier of coal to the Chicago, Burlington and Quincy Railroad.

In 1882, the CB&Q hired him to investigate the coal resources of Colorado. Osgood visited nearly every coal mining operation in the state and surveyed known coal deposits. His travels eventually brought him to the area of the Grand Hogback, and he came upon the valley of a river then known as Rock Creek, later to be called the Crystal River.

The valley of Rock Creek had been opened to prospecting in 1880, after the ouster of the Ute Indians. Walter Devereux had proven the existence of extensive coal reserves to the west of the Roaring Fork Valley. Devereux had filed claims on many of the deposits, developing them himself or leasing them to others. He became a very wealthy man in the process and went on to become the driving force behind much of the development of Glenwood Springs.

Walter Devereux and his family. Devereux was instrumental in the development of coal mining in western Colorado, and was responsible for the construction of the Hot Springs Pool and the Hotel Colorado in Glenwood Springs.
(Courtesy of Frontier Historical Society)

When John Osgood first visited that part of Western Colorado which was to become his home, he saw a region that showed signs of uncommonly varied mineral production. There were gold and silver mines, deposits of lead and copper and zinc, along with bituminous coal, and from all appearances, almost inexhaustible marble deposits on up the Crystal River. He formed the Colorado Fuel Company in Denver in 1884. Initially, the personnel of the company consisted of himself and a young office boy. By the beginning of 1884, Osgood controlled about 700 acres of coal land, and his company had a total capital of $50,000, an appreciable sum in the early 1880's. He spent the next four years acquiring coal deposits and operating mines in and around the Crystal River area. At about the same time, Osgood acquired options on many of the marble claims on Treasure Mountain, near the town of Marble, helping that fledgling industry to get off the ground. He also opened a coal mine near Crystal. In about 1888, he reorganized the company with $5,000,000 in capital. At that time, he controlled over 5,600 acres of coal land. John Osgood was becoming a dominant figure in the western coal industry.

Two miners named G. D. Griffith and W. D. Parry had filed a claim on what they hoped would be gold and silver producing property close to the headwaters of Coal Creek, north of its confluence with the Crystal River. While they owned it, a massive avalanche uncovered an impressive seam of coal. They did nothing to develop the claim, and ultimately sold it to John Osgood for $500. When the mine was initially opened, the coal was found to be of prime "coking" quality. The mine was to produce over a million tons of coal in the years between 1900 and 1909.

Coke is a fuel product that is created by heating bituminous, or "soft" coal under low oxygen conditions. In the late 1800's, this was accomplished in coke "ovens", beehive shaped structures of firebrick. The remaining ovens may still be seen along Highway 133, the interior edges of the firebrick fused into an almost glass-like surface by the great

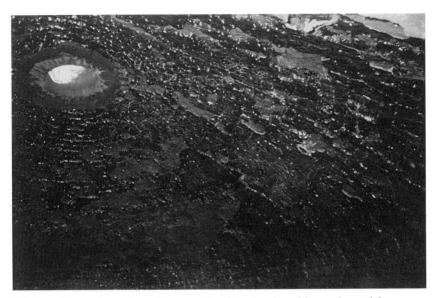

The interior surface of a coke oven, showing the glass-like surface of the firebrick, melted by the heat of the coking process. (Photo by the author)

heat created in the coking process. The ovens had small doors in one side of the base, and a ventilation hole at the top. The coal would be finely crushed and about three tons loaded into each oven. After the coal was ignited, the burning of the released gases maintained the heat, gradually transforming the coal into coke. The coal would initially soften, giving off coal tars and the gases, then solidify into a porous mass. In the early days of coking operations, the tar and gas were considered to be waste products. The process took about forty-eight hours. The resultant coke was a valued fuel that burned hot, giving off very little smoke. It was widely used in the smelting of metals, iron in the steel mills of the eastern United States and in Pueblo, Colorado, and silver in the mining camps of the west.

Osgood hired J. A. Kebler, Alfred Cass, David Beaman, and J. L. Jerome to assist him in the running of the reorganized company. They continued to acquire large tracts of coal land, operate the mines, and began acquiring and forming subsidiary companies such as the Crystal River Toll Road

Company. Osgood recognized the necessity of a means to transport the coal from his mines.

Another large company, the Colorado Coal and Iron Company, was also operating in the Crystal River Valley. The rival company, headed by William J. Palmer, was very prominent in the western fuel industry. As the only steel manufacturer west of the Mississippi, Colorado Coal and Iron was attempting to make Pueblo, Colorado the "Pittsburgh of the West" In July of 1886, they formed the Aspen and Western Railway to service their Thompson Creek mine. Three days later, Osgood incorporated the Crystal River Toll Road Company for the same purpose. Two of the giants in the fuel industry were about to engage in a battle for superiority.

The fight went on for several years, Colorado Coal and Iron and Colorado Fuel Company fighting for coal and railroad contracts. Osgood's company proved to be the more successful and profitable of the two, and a merger was proposed. At that time, Col. Channing F. Meek headed Colorado Coal and Iron. He was later to become the driving force behind the development of the marble quarries a few miles on up the valley. William Palmer, unhappy with the terms of the merger, dropped out of CC&I.

In 1892, the two companies were merged into Colorado Fuel and Iron, which was to become the most powerful fuel company in the western United States. Osgood, installing himself as the head of the new company, now controlled 69,000 acres of coal land, over 2,300 acres of iron land, 38 mining camps and rolling mills, 14 working mines, and 800 coke ovens in 4 locations.

At the age of 42, John Cleveland Osgood had become the "Fuel King of the West", and a multi-millionaire.

CHAPTER 3

THE MINING CAMPS - "COMPANY TOWNS"

The conditions under which coal miners worked and lived in Colorado have been described as atrocious. A great many of the miners came from other countries, most notably Italy, Czechoslovakia, Greece, and Austria. They were brought into the United States to work the coal mines after 1884-1885, when labor disputes with the American workers arose because of working conditions. Most of the immigrants were under a contractual obligation to their employer. In many cases, "brokers" would pay their transportation costs to the United States and guarantee to the Immigration Authorities that they would be gainfully employed. In return, the brokers received an assignment of the miner's wages until the transportation costs plus a large profit were paid.

Since the majority of the miners could not afford to bring their families with them, it was a lonely existence. It was therefore vital that they work to the satisfaction of the owners. Such things as sick leave, medical benefits, unemployment insurance or paid vacations did not exist for the miners. If a worker was unable to produce, he would simply be replaced. If he dared to complain about his lot, he might be fired, beaten, or blacklisted. There were instances of men leaving their family and their native land and subsequently dying in a cave-in or an explosion. The families of these unfortunates might never learn the fate of their loved one.

Since most of the coal mines were located some distance from established towns, the coal companies set up "company" towns to provide the essentials of life to their workers and their families, if and when their families were able to join them. The companies provided housing, schools, and usually some sort of recreational facilities, which might include bars, lounges, and game rooms. However, these towns were a form of trap for many of the miners.

In most of the coal towns, the housing for the miners

Photo in front of the "Club" in Coalbasin. Coalbasin was said to have three seasons - July, August, and winter. (Courtesy of Frontier Historical Society)

and their families consisted of little more than shacks, with no thought of any sort of indoor plumbing or insulation against the frigid winds of the high country. Coalbasin, the coal town nearest to present-day Redstone, sits at around 10,000 feet in elevation. It was said to have three seasons; July, August, and winter. In many of the towns, the lack of sanitation led to outbreaks of typhoid fever. Measles, mumps, and whooping cough tormented many of the children of the camps, and the infant mortality rate was high.

The miners and their families were not in fact owned by the coal companies, at least not in a legal sense. However, that was the sort of relationship that existed. Essentially every aspect of their lives was affected by the company. Their housing, their food, the schools, saloons, doctors, ministers, and most government officials were under the control of their employer; the miners had little in the way of legal rights. The fact that so many different nationalities were represented worked to the benefit of the coal companies; the lack of a common language helped to prevent

Coal mine tipple at Coalbasin around 1905. (Courtesy of Frontier Historical Society)

collaboration among the miners. Working in a hazardous environment next to someone who spoke a different language naturally added to the danger, but that factor did not seem to worry the mine owners.

The average miner earned about $3.00 per 12 hour day underground. To add to the aspect of control over the workers, the coal companies paid the men at least partially in script, redeemable only at the company stores. Using their minimal cash to purchase any sort of goods elsewhere was frowned upon.

Coal mining was always hazardous, and the coal mines of the Rocky Mountains were especially unforgiving. The extreme angles of the coal seams produced difficult working conditions in many of the mines. Heavy machinery and the explosives used to loosen the coal carry with them the threat of injury. Coal dust may be explosive, and its inhalation

*The 1907 snowslide that buried the company store and some of the miners'
houses at Coalbasin.* (Courtesy of Frontier Historical Society)

*The log building that was the original lantern house at Coalbasin. It i now
used as the Redstone Historical Museum.* (Photo by the author)

may result in black lung disease. Coal mines tend to produce noxious gases, most notably methane. Methane explosions touched off by sparks from machinery or simply from metal tools have caused the injury or death of many miners. Working far underground in tunnels may result in cave-ins or rockfalls, trapping or crushing the miners. "Bumps" or "bounces" may result from removing rock and coal from within the mountain. When the earth rearranges itself to accommodate the voids, it can move with incredible force. Depending on the severity of the movements, they can range from bothersome to lethal.

The attitudes of the employers and the resultant treatment of the miners naturally varied from company to company, but most indications are that the life of the coal miner in turn-of-the-century Colorado was a difficult one.

CHAPTER 4

OSGOOD TAKES A WIFE - OR TWO

By 1891, John Osgood was well on his way to controlling both coal and steel production in the mountain west. He was worth a great deal of money, and he either owned or controlled a large portion of the Crystal River Valley. He had built the Crystal River Ranch on the south bank of the river above the present site of Redstone. The ranch included a generating plant which provided electricity for the ranch and eventually the "Redstone Castle" and the town of Redstone. There was a two car siding and a small roundhouse off of the Crystal River Railroad for his private railroad car, named "Sunrise", and a dining car. The private cars boasted a porter and a cook with a wooden leg. Osgood frequently used the rail cars to travel to and from Redstone. In later years, Osgood was to incur the wrath of residents of Marble and of *The Marble Booster* for exercising what he apparently felt were his prerogatives in the use of the railroad. On at least one occasion, the normal schedule for the train from Carbondale to Marble was delayed for most of a day so that Osgood's private cars could come from Denver, travel on to Redstone, and return to Carbondale. The delay of the passengers, the mail, and the freight incensed the populace of Marble. Frank Frost, the editor of the *Booster,* wrote an uncharacteristically scathing editorial about it, calling Osgood a "bloated aristocrat".

Future outrages notwithstanding, Osgood was ready for a wife. In 1891, he met and married a lady who called herself Nonnie Irene de Belote, who was 20 years younger. They were married in New York. Her background prior to her marriage to Osgood is somewhat of a mystery. She told some people that she had been born on the Home Plantation in Virginia, while telling others, mostly people from Colorado, that she was from England. Interestingly, there is no record of a Home Plantation anywhere in Virginia, and there is likewise no record of the family name of Belote in England during that period. She was born in 1869, but in later years moved her birth date to 1875. The fact that the new birth date would have given her an age of 16 when she married John Osgood did not seem to concern her.

Nonnie Irene de Belote Osgood - John's first wife. She was a published author of romance novels. (Courtesy of Denver Public Library - Western History Collection)

Mrs. Osgood, known as Irene, was an intimidating woman, given to rather boisterous behavior and traveling with the late 1800's equivalent of the "jet set". She was a published author of romantic poetry and essays, and Osgood is said to have created the Cleveland Publishing House in New York to publish her work and that of her friends. Shortly after their marriage, she published her first novel, *Shadow of Desire.* There is some evidence that the novel is somewhat autobiographical, in that her heroine honeymooned at Trapper's Lake on the Flattops north of Glenwood Springs. Osgood had established a guest facility at Trapper's Lake, and it is possible that he and Irene did honeymoon there.

Early in their marriage, Irene made it clear to Osgood that she had no intention of moving to the "wilderness of Colorado" with him. He did convince her to set up residence in the new Hotel Colorado in Glenwood Springs. The luxurious hotel, considered to be one of the finest in the western part of the country, apparently met with her approval. According to local legend, however, her behavior was not considered to be quite appropriate by the management of the hotel. The story goes that she evidently became a bit too exuberant in her enjoyment of the hotel's bar - some would say that she was "rowdy and obnoxious" - and she was invited to leave. There is some question as to whether the issuer of the invitation fully realized who she was, but in any event, John Osgood was allegedly enraged.

Irene apparently did not let the fact of her marriage interfere with her idea of the good life. She moved freely about Europe and America, with or without her husband. A fellow author by the name of Robert Harborough Sherard seemed to command a good deal of her attention. The Cleveland Publishing House published one of his novels and another of Irene's in 1893. Hers, *Shadow of Desire,* was reviewed by the *New York Times.* The review, almost wholly uncomplimentary, concluded by saying that "The book is as unwholesome as any we have had the bad fortune to read."

Shortly thereafter, Osgood hired the architectural firm of Boal and Harnois of New York to begin the design of a mansion just below his ranch in the Crystal River Valley. As the designs were taking shape, Irene chose to run off with a Captain Charles Pigott Harvey, who eventually became her second husband. The Osgoods divorced, but he then circulated the story that she had been killed in New York's Central Park by a runaway horse. Even though the story was published in the *New York Times*, it was quite obviously untrue, but Osgood and his family stuck with it. In fact, Irene died in 1922.

John Osgood had met a lady by the name of Alma Regina Shelgrem some years previously, at the court of King Leopold of Belgium. He had been in Belgium attempting to enlist financial support from the King. Osgood apparently remained impressed by Alma, a tall, slender honey-blonde. She was quite attractive, and never denied reports that she came from Swedish royalty.

In 1899, he arrived in Denver with Alma Shelgrem and one of her friends. Denver society was all abuzz about a rumored scandal involving Alma, her girlfriend, and a certain

John Osgood proudly offers his hand to his second wife, Alma. She was later to become known as "Lady Bountiful," due to her kindness toward the people of Redstone. (Courtesy of Denver Public Library - Western History Collection)

Arthur Cobb of New York City. Cobb had apparently shot himself after leaving a note blaming Alma for his distress. The scandal was the apparent reason why Alma was snubbed by the "Sacred Thirty-Six", the informal association of 36 of Denver's most influential families. (This same group of self-important socialites was to later ostracize "The Unsinkable" Molly Brown, due to her "rough and uncouth" behavior.) Osgood was greatly displeased, and according to one source, he blamed his business associate, J. L. Jerome, for the snub. If true, the incident no doubt added to the spark of discord which was to grow between the two men. Disagreements over financial dealings and other areas of conflict drove a wedge between the two men that was never to fully disappear.

Osgood's divorce from Irene was final by 1899, and he married Alma in October of that year. Construction of the mansion began shortly thereafter. The fashion of the day was to name one's mansion, and the castle on the banks of the Crystal River was to be known as "Cleveholm". "Cleve" was John Cleveland Osgood's nickname, and "holm" is Swedish for "home in the country".

Cleveholm, John Osgood's castle in the Crystal River Valley. (Photo by the author)

CHAPTER 5

CLEVEHOLM - THE KING BUILDS HIS CASTLE

John Osgood chose a magnificent setting for his mansion. About a mile downstream from his ranch, he owned a 4,200 acre piece of property which included a meadow that sloped gently toward the Crystal River. The feudal lords of Europe traditionally located their homes some distance from the houses of their serfs. Coincidentally, the home of the feudal lord of Redstone was also located one aristocratic mile from the town that housed his workers.

Cleveholm, in its park-like, 4,200-acre setting a mile above Redstone.
(Courtesy of Frontier Historical Society - Shutte Collection)

The style of the day, for the American aristocrats, was to shamelessly flaunt their wealth. For many, that took the form of immense homes, sometimes several of them. To those

born to wealth, the trappings were important. To the new
rich, the breed of self-made millionaires, the evidence of
wealth was vital. Many of the barons of industry and their
wives and families lived lives of almost unbelievable luxury;
John and Alma Osgood were certainly no exception.

The red cliffs near the town yielded the blocks of stone
for the exterior of the house. Stonemasons were imported
from Europe to cut and fit the reddish sandstone blocks. The
style and exterior appointments were said to have been modeled after the Tudor manors of England. In fact, Theodore
Boal, of the architectural firm of Boal and Harnois, designed
the unique style of the mansion, the Inn, and the other buildings of the "Estate". The "castle" was designed to contain
some 42 rooms and 8 bathrooms. Fourteen fireplaces were
included to heat the place, and many of the draperies were
lined with insulating material. The mansion was to be
roughly 25,000 square feet in size. It wrapped around three
sides of a large courtyard which contained a marble water

*Marble water trough with the dragon fountain in the main courtyard of
Cleveholm.* (Photo by the author)

trough fed by a fountain in the shape of a dragon. The trough was carved from white marble and was presented to Osgood as a gift from the nearby Yule Marble Company. The trough was so heavy that a specially reinforced wagon was used to haul it the 12 miles to Cleveholm. To the right of the mansion was a large patio which overlooked the park-like meadow. An exceptionally persistent local legend has it that guests who were so inclined, could sit on the patio and shoot elk, deer, or mountain sheep. One of the buildings on the other side of the Crystal River housed the gamekeeper, who tended to the penned herds. According to the legend, the game would be driven across the huge lawn at the whim of the Osgoods or their visitors to provide targets for the "hunters".

It is true that the gamekeeper did keep herds of deer and elk in his pens, as was the fashion of the western aristocrat in those days. However, there is no proof whatsoever that this form of "hunting" ever occurred. In fact, John

One of Osgood's carriages. (Photo by the author)

Osgood spent tens of thousands of dollars on his private "zoo", building pens and water systems for the animals, and raising hay for their consumption. It is doubtful that any of Osgood's "pets" were subjected to that type of sport. In addition to the house of the gamekeeper, there were other buildings and residences scattered about the estate. The main gate, toward the river, was watched over by a gatekeeper, as was the rear gate up the hill. Each had their own house, whose design and opulence mirrored the mansion itself. Near the main gatekeeper's house was the carriage house, which sheltered an assortment of fancy carriages and Osgood's 1904 Pope Winton electric car. Osgood's expensive herd of horses also lived there, their stalls lined in fir paneling. Other buildings included a summer house, the coachman's residence, a hose house, a large greenhouse, and a kennel. There was a pagoda near the river where summer lawn concerts were presented for the enjoyment of the Osgoods and their guests. An intricately designed hand-wrought iron fence surrounded the courtyard.

The interior of the house reflected the wealth and the taste of the Osgoods. John and Alma traveled the world, gathering massive, ornate furniture to be shipped back to their home. Italian artists hand-stenciled various of the linen walls inside the mansion. One legend has it that a diamond dust mirror in Alma's bedroom cracked, and that one of the artists spent a great deal of time painting vines and flowers over the crack. Supposedly, she and the artist became involved in certain activities which had nothing at all to do with painting. A secret passageway which led from the servant's quarters to a door near her bedroom added to the legend. John Osgood, according to the story, found out about the affair and conveniently had the man shot during a poker game. True or not, modern-day guests who acknowledge a sensitivity to ghosts have reported a degree of discomfort upon entering the basement game room where the shooting supposedly happened.

Each of the rooms was decorated in its own manner, but

President Theodore Roosevelt. There is some disagreement as to whether he was an occasional guest of the Osgoods. (Courtesy of Frontier Historical Society)

each door was adorned with a brass knob. The connecting doors were faced with materials which would match the decor of their corresponding rooms. One door, for instance, might be oak on one side, to match the woodwork of the library, and mahogany on the other side to fit with the trim of the drawing room. The fireplaces were each faced with a different color of marble or other decorative stone.

The ceiling and the upper walls of the library were covered with hand-tooled, gold-inlaid leather. There is a theory that the green leather on the walls is elephant hide, but there is no proof of that. The library ceiling was covered in gold leaf and opaque stenciling, made by pounding pieces of pure gold between layers of leather until the thickness was that of cigarette paper. It was then pressed onto the linen covered plaster ceiling in small sheets.

The library of Cleveholm. The ceiling is covered in green leather, some say elephant hide, and embellished with gold leaf. (Photo by the author)

The drawing room or main living room was some 37 feet by 42 feet, and was overlooked by balconies on either side of a massive two story stone fireplace. The stone of the fireplace displays an intricately carved representation of the Osgood coat of arms, featuring a lion holding a sheaf of wheat, the symbol of free-born landed gentry, and a Latin inscription which translates as "Pure of Heart". The bronze andirons reflect the light from the large windows which look over the vast lawn toward the Crystal River and Mount Casa, across the valley. The three brass chandeliers were designed and produced by Tiffany's, and one version has it that the molds were broken after their manufacture. The furniture was of hand-carved oak and satin brocade. A small window set high in the wall opposite the door to the library was Alma's "peering window". Supposedly, she would peek at arriving guests in order to determine their manner of dress before she finalized her own dressing process.

The music room featured French style padded green silk brocade wall coverings and embroidered silk brocade furniture. A large diamond dust mirror reflected the thousands of crystal droplets of the chandelier, which hung from the middle of a wreath of cupids frescoed onto the ceiling.

Osgood's formal dining room was decorated in Russian style, with deep red velvet walls above dark mahogany wood. The original table and chairs were also dark mahogany. The ceiling of the dining room was covered in gold leaf, and a huge china cabinet displayed Havilland and Dresden china and crystal goblets through its curved glass. The fireplace in the dining room is faced in red marble from Carrera, Italy.

John's and Alma's separate bedrooms were of course decorated in the same opulent manner as the rest of the mansion. Massive oak or mahogany furniture, hand-carved

The drawing room, showing the Tiffany lamps and Lady Bountiful's "peering window," just behind and above the far chandelier. (Photo by the author)

or inlaid, and the finest of fabrics adorned the sleeping rooms. In keeping with the fact that John Osgood was a rather private individual who preferred smaller groups of people, there were only five guest bedrooms. Each of the guest rooms was decorated with the same elegance as the rest of the huge home. One wing contained ten smaller rooms, decorated somewhat less lavishly. These were the servant's quarters, the valet's room, and the watchman's room. The back part of the house, connected by stairways to the servant's bedrooms, contained the kitchen, the butler's pantry, and the servant's dining room. The lower level, which opened on the front lawn, contained Osgood's offices, the game room, a bar, a wine cellar, and a large vault. There were also servant's rooms on that level.

This massive bed is in John Osgood's bedroom. John and Alma Osgood traveled the world, gathering furnishings and appointments for their home. (Photo by the author)

Some estimates place the cost of construction of the estate at over three million dollars. In fact, the mansion itself probably cost around two hundred and fifty thousand, and

This is the fireplace in John Osgood's home. Each of the fireplaces in the mansion was faced with a different stone. (Photo by the author)

The "sun porch" of the castle - now used to serve breakfast to overnight guests. (Photo by the author)

the cost of the entire estate plus the town of Redstone likely totaled around two and a half million. That was a tremendous amount of money in the days that the miners were earning three dollars a day. It is also interesting to note that the State Capital Building of Colorado had cost just under three million dollars to complete a few years earlier.

After the completion of the mansion, the Osgoods entertained such notables as John D. Rockefeller, Jr., J. Pierpont Morgan, King Leopold of Belgium, and, possibly, President Teddy Roosevelt. At that time, the top of McClure Pass was accessible by a rough trail negotiable only on foot or horseback. One of Osgood's guests remarked that, in his opinion, a motorcar would never reach the summit of the pass. The next morning, the guests were treated to a horseback trip up the pass. To their amazement, sitting in a clearing at the very top of the pass was Osgood's automobile. He had instructed some of his men to dismantle the car, haul it up the pass, and reassemble it.

The entertainment offered to the guests of course included a tour of Redstone, the tidy little village which Osgood had created for his workers.

CHAPTER 6

REDSTONE - THE SOCIOLOGICAL EXPERIMENT

By the time he built his castle, John Osgood controlled many coal towns. Conditions under which the miners and their families lived varied, but they were almost invariably bad. Osgood had built a town at Coal Basin to house and provide necessities for the workers at the mine there. The residences there were well above average, neat rows of cabins with steeply-pitched roofs. Coalbasin had a bar and a game room for the workers, as well as a company store.

The coal produced at the Coal Basin mine was of excellent coking quality. Osgood's railroad hauled the coal down

Train on the "highline" from Redstone to Coalbasin. (Courtesy of Frontier Historical Society)

to the Crystal River, where 200 coking ovens had been constructed. Originally, the employees who operated the ovens had followed tradition and thrown up shacks near their work for shelter. It was obvious that this sort of thing could not be allowed to exist near Osgood's home. It was, therefore, with a great deal of enthusiasm that John Osgood threw himself into the design and building of their model company town.

The town of Redstone was to be the jewel of the Colo-

The remains of two of the beehive-shaped coke ovens at Redstone. Only the inner firebricks remain. (Photo by the author)

rado Fuel & Iron coal towns and the showplace of the Osgoods. By 1902, it had become known as "The Ruby of the Rockies". It was to be the centerpiece of John Osgood's great social experiment. Whereas the prevalent attitude toward the social welfare of workers in the coal industry was one of indifference, bordering on neglect, Osgood professed to view the situation totally differently. According to him, if his workers were kept happy and contented, they would stay with him regardless of such things as labor strikes. The coal industry had been subject to a good deal of unrest in the years leading up to 1900, mostly because of conditions under which the miners worked and lived. John Osgood intended to change all that, by providing clean, modern homes for his workers and their families. With his own money and that of CF&I available, John Osgood set out to create his showplace.

On July 25, 1901, it was announced that Dr. Richard Corwin had been appointed as head of the newly formed so-

The cliffs above town that gave Redstone its name. Note the line of coke ovens at the lower left. (Courtesy of Frontier Historical Society - Shutte Collection)

ciological department for CF&I. It was Dr. Corwin's job to look after Osgood's workers. It is unsure whether it was the influence of Corwin, the prompting of his wife, or a change in John Osgood's attitude toward his miners that brought about the humanitarian treatment of the workers who had been abused for so long. Whatever the reason, the initial response from the workers was one of surprise, followed by a grateful acceptance of their new lot in life.

When completed, Redstone boasted amenities that did not normally exist in company towns. There was a theater,

Second from the left is Dr. Richard Corwin, head of the Sociological Department of Colorado Fuel and Iron. John Osgood is third from the right. (Courtesy of Denver Public Library - Western History Collection)

complete with dressing rooms, lights, scenery, and an arc lighted stereopticon. A library with books and works of art was donated by the Osgoods. The miner's clubhouse was the scene of parties, dances, lantern shows, concerts, and lectures. It had a billiard room, a card room, and a reading room, and was also used for afternoon social functions by the women of the town, such as card parties or teas. The town also contained the depot, a post office, an assay office, and a blacksmith shop. The company store, operated by a subsidiary of CF&I, carried groceries, cooking utensils, and work clothing.

Two hotels were built to serve visitors to the fledgling town. The Redstone Inn was built primarily to house bachelor miners. It is commonly said to have been modeled after a Dutch Tavern, but it was again the creation of Theodore Boal. The Inn, a full service hotel which also catered to traveling salesmen, is adorned with a tower which houses a large clock on each of its four sides. The Inn originally had fourteen or so rooms. Like the remainder of Redstone, it was of first class construction, and provided quite comfortable quarters for the unmarried men. The other hotel, the Big Horn Lodge, was more opulent in design, catering to members of the CF&I Board of Directors and overflow guests of the Osgoods. It offered the best in food and service. Some sources, however, state that the lodge was on occasion rendered unusable due to fumes and smoke from the nearby coke ovens. One source, in fact, insists that the lodge was used only once for a meeting.

The Colorado Supply Co's Store No. 24, Redstone, Colo.

The Colorado Supply Company's Store No. 24 in Redstone. Photo from about 1906. (Courtesy of Frontier Historical Society)

The Redstone Inn, originally built as bachelor quarters for Osgood's miners, is now a full-service hotel and restaurant. (Courtesy of Denver Public Library - Western History Collection)

Osgood provided his village with a large, modern school, which included a kindergarten, a domestic science department, and manual training classes. The rooms were large and well lit, with adjustable desks and slate blackboards. Modern lavatories with hot and cold running water were provided.

The community was well equipped with electrical service, a quite efficient gravity-fed water system, and a fully equipped fire department. The firefighters had both a regular water hose cart and a carbon dioxide chemical cart. The firehouse even contained an exercise room for the firemen.

As impressive as the other buildings were, the collection of worker's houses really set Redstone apart from the remainder of the mining towns in the rest of turn-of the century America. More than eighty cottages were constructed, all with running water; the larger ones even had indoor bathtubs. The neat little houses were painted a variety of pastel colors, and many were surrounded by board fences. Each had a lawn and a small garden plot for the use of the occu-

The school in Redstone - provided by John Osgood for his miners and their families. (Courtesy of Denver Public Library - Western History Collection)

pants, and a community garden added to the vegetable growing capacity of the families. Each month, the most attractive yard earned an award for the responsible family. A communal herd of milk cows was kept in a pasture outside of town, and driven to a common barn each evening for milking. For thirty-five cents per lamp per month, electricity could be purchased. Bathing facilities were provided at the clubhouse, and the men were encouraged to bathe and change into clean clothing before going home to their neat little houses.

A community brass band was organized, the instruments having been donated by the Osgoods. There was an Italian bandmaster, and the members were required to pay dues of fifty cents a month, so that they would feel a part of the group.

Dr. Corwin, in his post as company sociologist, determined that a major social problem existed among the miners. In his opinion, the abuse of alcohol was one of the chief causes of absenteeism, as well as a causal factor in work accidents. He convinced Osgood that the controlling of alcoholic beverages would be a worthwhile move. The workers were accustomed to making their own beer and wine, and drunkenness was a problem. It is said that in Coalbasin, the miners brought four kegs of whiskey, eight kegs of beer, and a large quantity of wine into town, in anticipation of the Fourth of July. The entire camp was incapacitated for most of a week.

One of the surviving cottages that Osgood built for his miners and their families. (Photo by the author)

Osgood and Corwin instituted a policy in Coalbasin and Redstone. They allowed the clubhouses to serve liquor, but a "no treating" rule was applied. To paraphrase Osgood, "The club will sell beer, wine, and liquor to its members or visitors, but believing that each member has the intelligence to buy just what he wants, no treating will be allowed." In other words, a man could buy as many drinks for himself as he wanted, but he was not to be allowed to purchase a drink for anyone else. The system seemed to work, for the most part, but Corwin continued to speak out against strong drink.

The main street of Redstone, about 1905. (Courtesy of Al Maggard)

During the three year period when Redstone could be considered to be at its peak, the coke oven operators and their families lived in conditions rivaled in Denver by only a few of the wealthier homes and first class bordellos. Osgood was given awards for the results of his "experiment". We will never know for certain what John Osgood's intent was in providing uncommonly comfortable living conditions for the members of his "kingdom". We do know that he was heaped with both praise and scorn for his efforts. Even during the first three years of the century, when relationships with the workers were at their smoothest, some of the miners left Redstone to work the fruit orchards of Paonia, on the other side of McClure Pass. They left to seek a situation where they could feel more like "their own boss". When the miners went out on strike in 1903 in sympathy for eastern miners who were demanding recognition for the United Mine Workers, it marked the end of Osgood's "Grand Experiment". The experiment would later be branded as "paternalism at its worst", and Osgood would be criticized for denying the miners their "freedom".

LADY BOUNTIFUL - THE GUARDIAN ANGEL OF REDSTONE

Alma Regina Shelgrem may or may not have been a Swedish countess prior to coming to America with John Osgood. However, there does not seem to be any mention of her in the Swedish archives. To further add to the mystery, she was said to have traveled to France at the start of World War I, in order to establish a hospital on her estate for the American Red Cross. The French government, according to the story, tried to assassinate her because of her German connections.

Whatever her background, she was looked upon as a benefactor, a guardian angel, almost a saint by the people of Redstone. She and her husband doted on the town of their own creation like one would a favored child. There are theories that it was largely her influence that prompted Osgood to undertake the "Grand Experiment" in the first place.

There is little doubt that the people of Redstone, especially the children, loved her. There are many stories of her riding though the town in her carriage, asking if there was anything that anyone needed. If one of the residents required medical attention, for instance, she would see that it was provided. She was quick to see to any needs that the townspeople expressed. It was not long before someone, we shall never know who, referred to her as "Lady Bountiful". The name became her, and she became the name. Few who know anything of John Osgood and Redstone have any idea who Alma Shelgrem was, but they all know of Lady Bountiful.

Alma, or Lady Bountiful, served as wife and social hostess to her husband, helping to entertain their many influential guests. Being some years younger than her husband, she no doubt provided a degree of youthful enthusiasm to the social gatherings of the likes of the Goulds and the Rockefellers. She certainly fell into the role of wealthy

Alma Regina Shelgrem Osgood, known as "Lady Bountiful" by the people of Redstone. (Courtesy of Denver Public Library - Western History Collection)

industrialist's wife with a great deal of ease. In addition to serving as a gracious hostess, she also composed music. One of her compositions, the "Redstone Waltz", was of course about the place and the people that she loved.

A talented horsewoman and a crack shot, Mrs. Osgood was responsible for many of the hunting trophies presently displayed in Cleveholm. For instance, the large bear rug displayed in the game room of the castle was shot by Lady Bountiful in 1904. The bear, a 400 pounder, was the first of the season to be shot.

A cartoon appeared in the *Denver Post* in the very early years of the century, featuring a beautiful Victorian lady who rode around an unnamed town performing generous acts for the populace. Amazingly, the cartoon was called "Lady Bountiful".

She delighted in organizing lavish Christmas parties for the residents of Redstone and their children. She would see to it that the children's letters to Santa Claus were diverted to her, and talk to the parents regarding the children's Christmas wishes. She and John would then travel to Chicago and New York, purchase the gifts they had requested, and personally hand them out at the Christmas party. They were known to purchase gifts for each of the 400 citizens of Redstone.

Like many good things, the relationship between Lady Bountiful and the people of Redstone was not to last. It was not through any action of hers that the association ended, nor was it the fault of the people themselves. Rather, the change may be blamed on progress. John Osgood lost control of CF&I. Coal deposits were being discovered in more accessible sites, locations that did not depend on the whims of the weather to assure transportation of the product. Also, newer technologies had been developed for the coking of coal, techniques that allowed the capturing of the coal tars and gases that were wasted in the old beehive ovens. Thus, around 1909, the eyes of a still coal-hungry nation shifted away from Coalbasin and from Redstone.

In 1910, John Osgood and Lady Bountiful, as she was forever to be known, closed Cleveholm. They kept a small staff of servants to maintain the place, but Osgood himself was not to return for almost 14 years; Lady Bountiful was never to return. History is very sketchy regarding the last years of their marriage, but it is known that they did divorce sometime during that period. According to Osgood, their separate activities gradually pulled them apart. He did state, however, that she was one of the finest ladies he had ever known. As with his first marriage, there were no children.

At the same time the castle was closed, the town of Redstone was also all but abandoned. The mine and the coke ovens ceased operations. The tidy little mountain town was literally packed in mothballs; the empty houses were treated with mothballs to prevent damage to the draperies and floor coverings. Again, a skeleton staff of maintenance workers was retained to shovel snow off the roofs and to keep the water and electrical systems in repair. During the next decade, Redstone was probably history's most well kept ghost town.

Alma Regina Shelgrem Osgood, "Lady Bountiful" to the grateful populace of Redstone, Colorado, died in France in 1955.

THE END OF AN ERA

Even though John Osgood attained the title of "Fuel King of the West", that did not prevent other men of power and ambition from trying to dethrone him. He had historically been successful in maintaining control of his companies, and that control had allowed him to spend company funds for many of his building projects, land acquisitions, and social experiments. However, the strike of 1902 severely curtailed the abundant flow of cash to him and to CF&I. For the first time since taking over the huge coal and iron company, Osgood was forced to go to Wall Street seeking investors. This opened the door for those who would see him overthrown.

Another self-made millionaire by the name of John Warne Gates was to step forward and challenge John Osgood for control of CF&I. Gates had begun as a hardware salesman. Seeing the tremendous potential for barbed wire in a country just beginning to fence itself in, he gradually created a monopoly in the manufacture of barbed wire. By 1898 he had formed the American Steel and Wire Company. He became quite wealthy, and developed a reputation for extremely high-stakes gambling, both at the poker table and in the business world. He became known as John "Bet-A-Million" Gates.

When the CF&I stock became available on the open market, Gates quickly acquired a stock position second only to Osgood himself. Gates then demanded that Osgood sell out to United States Steel, who had offered to buy the CF&I stock at a price which would have afforded Gates a quick profit. When Osgood refused, Gates initiated a stock battle that ultimately resulted in a reduction in the stock price. Gates finally sold out to George Gould at a sizable loss. Biographers have placed Gate's loss at three million dollars in a two month period. Osgood had won that battle, but he was to lose the war. In fighting Gates, he had been forced to borrow several million dollars from John D. Rockefeller and from

George Gould. This action allowed Gould and Rockefeller to gain control of the company, and John Cleveland Osgood resigned from Colorado Fuel and Iron on June 24, 1903.

Osgood had personally developed the Victor-American Fuel Company while still the head of CF&I, and he now turned his energies toward the further development of that company. J. L. Jerome, one of his partners in CF&I, soon found that he was not to share in the profits of Victor-American, even though he had originally loaned his own money toward the development. He threatened to sue Osgood, but all three of Osgood's partners in Victor-American died within the next five months; Kebler of a heart attack, Cass of a stroke, and Jerome by suicide. The split between Osgood and Jerome, which was caused by disputes over money and the shunning of Alma by the "Sacred Thirty-Six" in Denver, had never healed.

In typical fashion, Osgood built Victor-American into the second ranking fuel company in Colorado, second only to Colorado Fuel and Iron, his old company. However, neither company was ever to regain the glory of the old coal industry; natural gas and petroleum were making inroads into the energy field. While coal was to remain a major fuel source, especially for the metallurgical industries, the old mining methods and the beehive shaped coke ovens were becoming antiquated, obsolete. The mine and the town of Coalbasin were both abandoned by late 1909. The town stood vacant for years, and the furniture and buildings were gradually hauled off. No trace of the old coal mining town now remains.

During the next several years, the coal industry was hurt by repeated strikes. The confrontations between the enforcers of the coal company owners and the striking miners became known as the "The Coalfield Wars of 1913-1914". The most serious incident was to occur near Ludlow, Colorado, on the eastern slope of the Rockies. Hostilities had escalated to the point of gunfire on several occasions. On April 20, 1914, the state militia attacked and burned a tent city housing strik-

The monument commemorating the site of the "Ludlow Massacre" in southeastern Colorado. (Photo by the author)

ing miners and their families.

A monument now stands at the site of what was to become known as the "Ludlow Massacre". The monument reads:

> *On April 20, 1914, the state militia unleashed an unwarranted attack on striking coal miners and their families living in a tent colony at this site. Eleven children and two women suffocated in a cellar beneath a tent when flames engulfed the overhead shelter. Militia rifle and machine gun fire claimed the lives of at least 5 strikers, an 11 year old boy, and an 18 year old passerby.*
>
> *The unexpected attack was the fateful climax of miners attempting to achieve freedom from oppression at the*

hands of coal company officials. Miners were forced to live in company owned camps, buy from company owned stores, and educate their children in company dominated schools. Miners worked unduly long hours under hazardous conditions for meager pay.

On Sept. 23, 1913, miners struck in protest of these conditions, calling for recognition of the United Mine Workers Union. Eventually, the alleged peace keeping militia became infiltrated with company gunmen, leading to this - the Ludlow Massacre.

UMWA L.U. 9856 Dist. 15

Little is known of Osgood's movements for the next ten years or so. It is known that he and Alma divorced sometime before 1920. He was not to reappear in western Colorado until 1924. When he did, it was in the company of his third wife. He had met Lucille Reid sometime between 1917 and 1920, and they were married in New York in November of 1920. Whereas the backgrounds of his first two wives were somewhat mysterious, Lucille's past was almost a complete unknown. It is known that she was born in Oakland, California, and that she was twenty-five years of age when they married.

Osgood was in his seventies by then, but he still possessed a great deal of money and the desire to maintain his "showplace". During the winter of 1924-25 and the summer of 1925, Redstone and the grounds of Cleveholm were alive with workmen, some 165 in all. They worked on the water system, the electrical wiring, and the grounds of the castle. A new generator was installed in the hydroelectric plant. By the end of the summer, the mansion, the Inn, and the town were approaching their original condition.

In the early winter of 1925, rumors began circulating about John Osgood's health. As it turned out, he was gravely ill with cancer. He was subjected to at least one operation in Denver. John Cleveland Osgood died on January 4, 1926 in his bedroom in the mansion that he had loved. He was cre-

A newspaper photo of Lucille Reid Osgood, John's third wife. Little is known of her background. (Courtesy of Denver Public Library - Western History Collection)

mated, and his ashes scattered near the mansion and the Crystal River.

Lucille continued to run Osgood's still many and varied business pursuits. He had willed to her all of his interests, including Victor-American Fuel, the Colorado Security Company, the Colorado Southeastern Road, real estate in Chicago and New York, and the townsites of Minnaqua and Redstone, as well as some four and a half million dollars in cash. Unfortunately, Lucille chose to burn many of his records, documents, and personal papers after his death, obliterating much of an already incomplete history of the man.

Lucille continued to live in Cleveholm for several years, tending to the remaining business interests and raising prize winning lettuce and potatoes. She married a Huntley McDonald sometime in the late 20's. It is theorized that her new husband invested most of her fortune in the stock market just in time for the crash of 1929. They reopened the Redstone Inn and attempted to promote Redstone and the Inn as a vacation resort. Their timing probably could have not been worse, coming as it did in the middle of the Great Depression which ran from 1929 to about 1940. Finally, in 1940, the Redstone Inn was sold to a Dr. Russell Gray. As time went on, more and more of the buildings on the estate and in the town itself were either sold and moved away or simply torn down for the building materials. The Bighorn Lodge, built to be the elegant lodging place for CFI's Board of Directors, was sold for $600 and dismantled. The south gate house was removed, stone by stone, and reassembled in a residential area of Grand Junction, Colorado. The greenhouse from the Cleveholm grounds was sold and moved to Glenwood Springs, where it now sits just off the frontage road between Glenwood Springs and West Glenwood. The school, many of the cottages, the depot, the post office, and the

The Cleveholm Manor greenhouse - now located in West Glenwood Springs, Colorado. (Courtesy of Frontier Historical Society)

miner's clubhouse were all torn down, to get them off the tax rolls.

The castle itself was finally sold to Ray and Lila Hibbert of Golden, Colorado in about 1946. They in turn sold it to Dean and Rose Cook, who operated it as a hotel under the name of Crystal River Lodge. They in turn sold it in 1958 to Glenwood Hotelier Frank Kistler, who changed the name to the Redstone Castle.

Ken Johnson, Grand Junction Daily Sentinel publisher, became the next owner of the castle in 1974. Johnson, an historian in his own right, spent a great deal of time researching and restoring the grand old mansion. The castle, the carriage house, and indeed the entire town of Redstone, is listed in the National Register of Historical Places.

Morgan Rothschild Co. of Canada purchased the property in 1997. Foreclosure proceedings were begun in February of 1999, and the castle closed its doors to the public in July of that year. An auction was set for August, and Redstone residents and business owners feared that the property might become a private residence.

Then, in early August of 1999, the castle, the adjacent carriage house, and the surrounding 159 acres of land was acquired by the Cumberland Fund, a Dallas-based investment group. The announced intention of the new owner was to renovate the old mansion and convert it into a high quality hotel and restaurant. However, those plans were not to come to fruition, and the Redstone Castle once again went up on the auction block on April 2, 2000.

CHAPTER 9

THE MINES REOPEN

By the 1950s, a series of mines had been reopened in the vicinity of Osgood's Coalbasin operation. They were operated by Mid-Continent Resources. The reopening of the mines helped to bolster Redstone's economy. Some of the miners resided in Redstone, as did employees of Morrison-Knudsen, the trucking company that hauled the coal to Carbondale. Mid-Continent was able to compete with more accessible mines because of dramatic advancements in coal mining operations. Most notable was the "longwall" method of mining. The longwall system originated in Europe and has become increasingly popular in the United States. In the early 1990s, longwall mining accounted for about one third of all United States coal produced underground, compared with only about 10 percent in 1980. In longwall mining, a rotating shear sweeps from side to side, cutting across the coal seam in an arc of 600 to 1,000 feet. The loosened coal falls onto a conveyor, where it is transported back away from the coal face. A hydraulic roof support system of shields or jacks supports the roof, advancing as mining proceeds and allowing the roof to gently fall, filling the resulting void in areas already mined.

The Mid-Continent Dutch Creek No. 1 mine was considered to be the most productive, but it also held extensive pockets of methane. It has been estimated that the No. 1 mine released 1.5 million cubic feet of methane each day. The mine was classified as "potentially hazardous", due to the high liberation of methane. Nine miners were killed in the tunnel of Dutch Creek No. 1 in a methane blast in 1965.

On April 15, 1981, 22 men were working in the Dutch Creek No. 1 mine. About 4:15 in the afternoon, there was a massive explosion some 7,200 feet from the surface. The blast knocked out both the ventilation system and communications system, making rescue efforts even more hazardous. A short time after the explosion, three men emerged from the mine entrance uninjured. Then, a rescue team brought out four more men, all alive but with varying degrees of burns or other injuries.

As families of the 15 men still missing set up a vigil around campfires on the mountainside below the mine entrance, rescue teams inched their way along the 13 degree slope toward the area of the explosion. Finally, a day and an half after the blast ripped through the lower reaches of the mine, nine of the miners were found. It appeared that they had died instantly. As one miner put it, "Being near a methane explosion in a mine shaft would be like being in an exploding gun barrel." About three hours later another five were found, and the fifteenth and last body was discovered another three hours later. The vigil of the families was at last over.

The Mid-Continent mines were re-opened shortly after the disaster, but have since been closed permanently. The area of the mines and the accompanying buildings has undergone extensive reclamation. The buildings have been demolished, scraps of metal and other foreign substances have been removed, and native vegetation has been replanted. Once again, Coal Basin looks much as it did when John Osgood first laid eyes on it.

The area of the Mid-Continent mine buildings, during reclamation. (Photo by the author)

CHAPTER 10

PRESENT DAY REDSTONE

The mines have closed, reopened for a period of time, and finally closed permanently. The coke ovens, the reason for the original population of Redstone, are silent. John Cleveland Osgood and Lady Bountiful are gone; they are no more than memories, but much of the world that they created in the Crystal River Valley remains. It is doubtful that they ever intended to build a tourist town, at least not in the usual sense, but that is in fact the way it turned out.

The Redstone Inn about 1950. The old inn has resumed service as a hotel and restaurant. (Courtesy of Frontier Historical Society - Shutte Collection)

The Redstone Inn was expanded to 42 rooms by Frank Kistler, and is a full service hotel and restaurant. It is a popular locale for weddings. Other lodging places such as motels and bed and breakfast operations have been constructed to house the influx of visitors. Cleveholm, the

Redstone Castle itself, once again changed hands. On April 2, 2000, the castle, the carriage house, and the grounds were auctioned. There was a very real fear that the property would be broken up, sold off for housing developments, closed forever to the public.

To the delight of the residents and merchants of Redstone, the entire parcel was purchased for the winning bid of six million dollars. Leon and Debbie Harte, representing an organization called Tranquil Options, made the successful bid. Tranquil Options has interests in wellness facilities in Canada and in Australia, as well as in New York restaurants.

The Hartes indicated that they plan to move into the carriage house and spend whatever time is necessary to restore the old mansion to its early glory. Long-term plans included the possibility of a wellness center, a bed and breakfast operation, or a restaurant. In the meantime, Leon Harte vowed that the Redstone Castle would remain open to the public for tours, weddings, and the like.

In his words, "It would be a total shame to hide this from the public. It's history!"

In Redstone, some of the original cottages have survived, and local historical preservation ordinances dictate what, if any, changes may be made to the exteriors of the houses. They are still painted in the pastel colors, and serve as functioning memorials to the original occupants.

Other homes have been constructed in and around Redstone, and most of them follow the Victorian era style of architecture. Many of the current residents are owners or employees of the various businesses in Redstone, but others make a daily commute to Carbondale, Glenwood Springs or Aspen to work. Also, a number of the residences in the area serve as summer homes, or to the more hardy retirees, year-round homes.

A number of gift and specialty shops, as well as eating and drinking establishments have appeared along the main street. Redstone has become a paradise for the tourist. It is

One of the surviving houses along the main street of Redstone. (Photo by the author)

Proof that some Redstone residents have a bit too much time on their hands. (Note the fins in the water around the "swimmer." (Photo by the author)

a town for walking. Visitors tend to wander up and down the few blocks of the main street, through the town park with its massive marble slab picnic tables, and to the bank of the Crystal River. Spring and summer offer clear days and cool nights, fall brings the gold of aspens against the red cliffs, and winter provides endless snowfields for the snowmobiler, the snowshoe enthusiast and the cross-country skier.

When the Ute Indians inhabited the Crystal River Valley, the hills surrounding the present site of Redstone abounded with wild game; elk, deer, bear, and mountain sheep grazed in the high meadows. Native Cutthroat and Brook trout navigated the streams and rivers in search of

Marble slab picnic tables in the Redstone city park. (Photo by the author)

the unwary insect or larvae. The Utes became quite adept at "harvesting" these furred or finned creatures, using bows and arrows, spears, or fishhooks carved from bone.

Today, it is not at all unusual to see a herd of deer working the meadows at dusk, or to spot a mountain sheep or two moving along the seemingly sheer cliffs above Redstone. Elk

Hays Creek Falls, just off Highway 133 between Redstone and Marble. (Photo by the author)

are more secretive, but their bugling mating calls may sometimes be heard in the hills above town.

Modern fishermen whip the waters of the Crystal River to a froth in their quest for the elusive trout. Each autumn, the woods around Redstone fill with orange-clad hunters in search of big game. Like the fishermen, their tools of the hunt are technologically far superior to those of the ancient hunters. Whether their success rate is also better is a matter for conjecture.

When early winter comes to the Crystal River Valley, time seems to slow down for a while. The tourists are largely gone, back home making money so that they may return next year. The golden foliage of the fall has darkened and fallen, and the clouds that blow in over Chair Mountain bring sleet or snow, rather than the rains of summer. The shops that remain open are quiet, and the park is covered in an unbroken layer of white. For a few weeks, Redstone resembles the ghost town that it tried to become early in the 20th century.

Then, the snows deepen, the pines and the bare limbs of the aspens collect more of their white decoration, and the winter sports enthusiasts appear. After its brief respite, Redstone once again prepares to play host to the world.

BIBLIOGRAPHY

BOOKS

Benson, Maxine. 1994. *1001 Colorado Place Names.* Lawrence: University Press of Kansas

Cassells, E. Steve. 1983. *The Archaeology of Colorado.* Boulder: Johnson Books

Ellis, Richard N. 1989. *The Ute Legacy.* Ignacio: Pinon Press

Foote, Alvin. 1950. *The Fabulous Valley.* New York: A. & T. Company, Inc.

Francis, Theresa V. 1959. Reprinted 1984. *Crystal River Saga.*

Gulliford, Andrew. 1983. *Garfield County, Colorado: The First Hundred Years 1883-1983.* Glenwood Springs: Gran Farnum Printing & Publishing CompanyMarsh, Charles S. 1982. *People of the Shining Mountains.* Boulder: Pruett Publishing Company

Hunt, Inez and Draper, Wanetta W. 1960. *To Colorado's Restless Ghosts.* Denver: Sage Books

Isler, Ruby. *Date History of Marble Colorado*

Johnson, Anna and Yajko, Kathleen. 1983. *The Elusive Dream.* Glenwood Springs: Gran Farnum Printing & Publishing Company

Kenney, Norma. 1992. *The Hidden Place - Redstone.* Redstone: Redstone Press

McCollum, Oscar Jr. 1992. *Marble - A Town Built on Dreams - Volume I.* Denver: Sundance Publications, Limited

McCollum, Oscar Jr. 1993. *Marble - A Town Built on Dreams - Volume II.* Denver: Sundance Publications, LimitedPettit, Jan. 1982. *Utes - The Mountain People.* Colorado Springs: Century One Press

McCoy, Dell. 1972. *The Crystal River Pictorial.* Silverton: Sundance Publications Limited

Ruland, Sylvia. 1981. *The Lion of Redstone.* Boulder: Johnson Books

Shoemaker, Len. 1973. *Roaring Fork Valley - An Illustrated Chronicle.* Sundance Publications, Limited

Urquart, Lena M. 1970. *Glenwood Springs: Spa in the Mountains.* Taylor Publishing Company

Vandenbusche, Duane and Myers, Rex. 1970. *Marble, Colorado - City of Stone.* Denver: Golden Bell Press

Werner, Fred H. 1985. *Meeker - The Story of the Meeker Massacre and Thornburgh Battle September 29, 1979.* Greeley: Werner Publications

ABOUT THE AUTHOR

I am, in real life, an accountant. Some 25 years ago, my wife, Mary, and I were fortunate enough to relocate from Denver to Western Colorado. To say that we have never regretted the move would be an understatement.

We fell in love with the area at first sight, and that love has grown over the past quarter century. We settled in Glenwood Springs, and immediately began to poke around the myriad scenic areas which surrounded our new home. From the beginning, the Crystal River Valley has been a favorite target for our explorations.

We immediately began hearing stories of the "Ute Curse", of the "Redstone Castle", of the abandoned marble quarry which had yielded the stone for the Lincoln Memorial, for the Tomb of the Unknown Soldier. The area obviously deserved further exploration.

My other published works include THE CASE OF THE BLUE CHICKEN, a satire of detective novels, and COMPULSIVE, a psychological fiction.

I have also published three other history books: A QUICK HISTORY OF GLENWOOD SPRINGS, GLENWOODS SPRINGS - A ROCKY MOUNTAIN RESORT, and GLENWOOD CAVERNS AND THE HISTORIC FAIRY CAVES.

Many people assisted me in compiling this history and the accompanying photos. My fervent gratitude to Oscar McCollum for reviewing the Marble portion of the manuscript, and to Ken Johnson for his input on Redstone. Special thanks to Willa Soncarty and Ann Roberts of the Frontier Historical Museum, as well as to the entire museum board. Thanks also to Sharon Graves, Bill Shettig, JoAn Mayes, Kay Lamire, Scott Leslie, and Ann Martin.